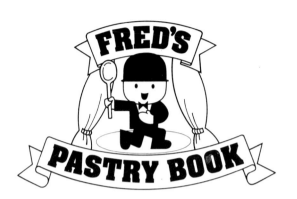

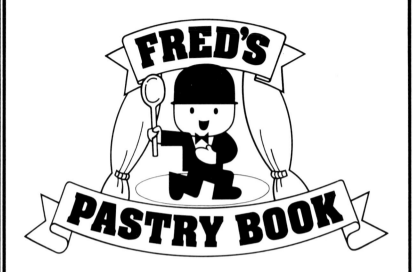

FRED'S PASTRY BOOK

HAMLYN

London · New York · Sydney · Toronto

Acknowledgements

The publishers would like to thank the following for their help
in sponsoring the colour photographs for this book:
The Homepride Kitchen: pages 18, 35, 36, 101, 102–3 and 104
Potato Marketing Board: page 92
Pointerware (U.K.) Limited: page 74
New Zealand Lamb Information Bureau: page 91
White Fish Authority: page 72
Meat Promotion Executive: page 71

Recipes compiled by Bridget Jones
Photography by Paul Williams
Edited by Carol Bowen

Illustrations by David Mostyn

Published by The Hamlyn Publishing Group Limited
London · New York · Sydney · Toronto
Astronaut House, Feltham, Middlesex, England
Text © Copyright The Hamlyn Publishing Group Limited
Line illustrations © Copyright Spillers Limited
'Fred the Flour Grader' is the trademark of
Spillers Limited of London, England 1981

ISBN 0 600 32245 9

Filmset in England by Tameside Filmsetting Limited,
Ashton-under-Lyne
Printed in Italy

Contents

Useful Facts and Figures

Notes on metrication

In this book quantities are given in metric and Imperial measures. Exact conversion from Imperial to metric measures does not usually give very convenient working quantities and so the metric measures have been rounded off into units of 25 grams. The table below shows the recommended equivalents.

Ounces	Approx g to nearest whole figure	Recommended conversion to nearest unit of 25
1	28	25
2	57	50
3	85	75
4	113	100
5	142	150
6	170	175
7	198	200
8	227	225
9	255	250
10	283	275
11	312	300
12	340	350
13	368	375
14	396	400
15	425	425
16 (1 lb)	454	450
17	482	475
18	510	500
19	539	550
20 (1¼ lb)	567	575

Note: When converting quantities over 20 oz first add the appropriate figures in the centre column, then adjust to the nearest unit of 25. As a general guide, 1 kg (1000 g) equals 2.2 lb or about 2 lb 3 oz. This method of conversion gives good results in nearly all cases, although in certain pastry and cake recipes a more accurate conversion is necessary to produce a balanced recipe.

Liquid measures The millilitre has been used in this book and the following table gives a few examples.

Imperial	Approx ml to nearest whole figure	Recommended ml
$\frac{1}{4}$ pint	142	150 ml
$\frac{1}{2}$ pint	283	300 ml
$\frac{3}{4}$ pint	425	450 ml
1 pint	567	600 ml
1$\frac{1}{2}$ pints	851	900 ml
1$\frac{3}{4}$ pints	992	1000 ml (1 litre)

Spoon measures All spoon measures given in this book are level unless otherwise stated.
Metric equivalents to the spoon sizes used are:
1 tablespoon = 1 × 15 ml spoon
1 teaspoon = 1 × 5 ml spoon
Can sizes At present, cans are marked with the exact (usually to the nearest whole number) metric equivalent of the Imperial weight of the contents, so we have followed this practice when giving can sizes.
Egg sizes All the recipes in this book have been tested using size 3 eggs.

Oven temperatures
The table below gives recommended equivalents.

	°C	°F	Gas Mark
Very cool	110	225	$\frac{1}{4}$
	120	250	$\frac{1}{2}$
Cool	140	275	1
	150	300	2
Moderate	160	325	3
	180	350	4
Moderately hot	190	375	5
	200	400	6
Hot	220	425	7
	230	450	8
Very hot	240	475	9

Notes for American and Australian users

In America the 8-oz measuring cup is used. In Australia metric measures are now used in conjunction with the standard 250-ml measuring cup. The Imperial pint, used in Britain and Australia, is 20 fl oz, while the American pint is 16 fl oz. It is important to remember that the Australian tablespoon differs from both the British and American tablespoons; the table below gives a comparison. The British standard tablespoon, which has been used throughout this book, holds 17.7 ml, the American 14.2 ml, and the Australian 20 ml. A teaspoon holds approximately 5 ml in all three countries.

British	American	Australian
1 teaspoon	1 teaspoon	1 teaspoon
1 tablespoon	1 tablespoon	1 tablespoon
2 tablespoons	3 tablespoons	2 tablespoons
$3\frac{1}{2}$ tablespoons	4 tablespoons	3 tablespoons
4 tablespoons	5 tablespoons	$3\frac{1}{2}$ tablespoons

An Imperial/American guide to solid and liquid measures
Solid measures

Imperial	American
1 lb butter or margarine	2 cups
1 lb flour	4 cups
1 lb granulated or castor sugar	2 cups
1 lb icing sugar	3 cups
8 oz rice	1 cup

Liquid measures

Imperial	American
$\frac{1}{4}$ pint liquid	$\frac{2}{3}$ cup liquid
$\frac{1}{2}$ pint	$1\frac{1}{4}$ cups
$\frac{3}{4}$ pint	2 cups
1 pint	$2\frac{1}{2}$ cups
$1\frac{1}{2}$ pints	$3\frac{3}{4}$ cups
2 pints	5 cups ($2\frac{1}{2}$ pints)

Note: When making any of the recipes in this book, only follow one set of measures as they are not interchangeable.

Foreword

Dear Friends,
My colleagues and I at Homepride have been busy working with Hamlyn Publishers to bring you this book on pastry making.

We do hope you enjoy reading it and trying all these mouth-watering recipes that have been developed in the Hamlyn and Homepride Kitchens.

We strongly recommend that you use Homepride Flour in all your baking and pastry making – as you know, Homepride Flour has always been the finest flour you can buy and this is a particularly important fact when it comes to pastry making.

You might say that with our fine flour and recipes and your fine baking we'll make some fine pastry!

FRED

Fred,
Chief Flour Grader

CHAPTER I

Introduction

Pastry is an ancient food; it was made by early oriental civilisations as well as the Greeks and Romans. The Orientals produced a basic mixture of flour and water to form a paste while more adventurous combinations of ingredients, similar to our own pastries, were produced by the Greeks. The first type of pastry made in Britain was probably similar to that of oriental origin, being a mixture of flour and water. This mixture was called huff paste and was wrapped around meat and poultry during cooking in order to preserve the flavour and juices. The paste was then discarded before serving the meat. Gradually it was realised that the paste absorbed the juices and flavour and it was eaten separately as a delicacy. As time went on, cooks enriched their pastes by the addition of fat and seasoning, thus making it more palatable so it could be eaten together with the food with which it was cooked.

Although the basic ingredients which are used in the making of pastry have remained the same for centuries, the different types of pastry which we know today have evolved through varying the type of ingredients and the proportions in which they are used. Short-crust pastry is the most popular and versatile pastry; puff, flaky and rough puff pastries require more preparation and are generally used for specialised dishes. Other pastries which are well known, although less frequently used, are the choux, suet and hot water crust varieties. The methods by which these pastries are prepared vary, however there are certain points to remember when choosing ingredients for making pastry.

Choice of Ingredients

Pastry is a mixture of flour, fat and liquid with the possible addition of sweetening, seasoning or other ingredients to enrich and give flavour.

Flour

There are many different types of flour available, ranging from the basic all-purpose plain or self-raising varieties to special strong, wholewheat or brown wheatmeal flours. All the recipes in this book have been tested using Homepride or Harvest Gold flours. Due to the fact that 'Homepride' flour has been pre-sifted, instructions for sifting flour have not been included in the recipes. If pre-sifted flour is not used it is recommended that white flour should be sifted before use.

The protein in flour combines with water to form gluten. Gluten is a tough, elastic substance which is important in determining the texture and structure of certain cooked foods, for example bread. The in-built strength of gluten is utilised to produce an elastic dough and give bread a light, open texture. This dough structure will not break down easily during cooking because, as the air expands or moisture vaporises, the mixture stretches to enclose it and eventually sets to maintain this framework. Strong flours have a higher proportion of gluten than weak or soft flours. The strength of the flour depends upon the wheat. Strong wheats have a higher protein content and therefore produce more gluten.

Since most cooked pastry should be light and crisp with a fairly crumbly texture, we generally use soft or weak flours for these, as opposed to the strong flours used to make bread. Most pastries are made using plain flour, the exception being suet crust pastry where self-raising flour is required to give lightness and texture. Due to the gluten content of strong flour and its ability to form a tough structure which traps air, it is useful in the making of puff, flaky and rough puff pastries. These pastries are not close textured but should be light and well risen with distinct layers. The extra strength provided by the gluten in strong flour means that the layers are less likely to break down and the air is easily trapped. By dampening the trays on which these pastries are baked steam is created during cooking, and this also helps to make the pastry rise. Choux pastry also rises more during cooking if strong flour is used though does tend to toughen. Since kneading helps to toughen the gluten, short pastry should be handled lightly and quickly. Similarly a little lemon juice may be added to the water used in puff pastry in order to strengthen the layers. The high proportion of fat to flour in pastry helps to weaken the gluten and give the required texture. The addition of sugar to a rich sweet pastry also weakens the effect of the gluten and in turn the structure. Therefore, it may generally be assumed that the weaker, all-purpose flours are most suitable for pastry-making and that they are usually plain rather than self-raising.

Fat

Butter, margarine, lard and suet are all used to make pastry as well as cooking fats specifically manufactured for making pastry, and cooking oil, which may be used in particular tested recipes. Butter and margarine give the best flavour while lard has better shortening properties. Suet is only recommended for use in suet crust pastry. The recipes in this book all use margarine, apart from hot water crust pastry which is made using lard, and suet crust pastry which uses suet. Some recipes suggest the use of butter (for example choux pastry and sweet flan pastry) as this improves the flavour of the pastry. For shortcrust, puff, flaky and rough puff pastries a combination of half lard and half margarine may be used instead of all margarine. This combination of fats will make the pastry slightly shorter, although the flavour is not as good.

Fats should be stored in a refrigerator or cool place and should not be kept for any great length of time as they will become rancid. They may, however, be stored in a freezer, which does not prevent their becoming rancid, but their storage life is extended to approximately 2 months. For recipes where the fat is rubbed in to the flour, the fat is best used straight from the refrigerator and should be cut into small pieces. Where fat is incorporated in the rolling process (as in puff and flaky pastries) it should be used straight from the refrigerator and margarine, if used, should be the hard type. If it is necessary to shape the fat before use (as for puff pastry), this should be done and the fat chilled again before use. Soft margarines are easier to rub into flour than the hard varieties.

Liquid

The rubbed-in ingredients are bound together with a liquid. In most recipes the liquid used is water, however, egg yolks are often used to enrich a pastry mixture. Water should be used sparingly in shortcrust pastry and, for recipes where the water is not heated, it should be used chilled or ice cubes should be added to reduce the temperature. The quantity of water used in shortcrust pastry is related to the behaviour of the protein in the flour. Since only a small quantity of water is added, the gluten is not developed so the pastry will be short.

Flavouring

Flavourings may be added to the pastry for use in certain recipes.

The addition of sugar is quite common for sweet, rich recipes and ground or chopped nuts may be used to vary both the flavour and texture of the pastry. Grated lemon and orange rind give an excellent flavour in both savoury and sweet dishes. Herbs and spices may also be used for flavour in sweet and savoury recipes. Finely-grated cheese may be added to the pastry for savoury dishes and this mixture can also be used to make cheese biscuits. A little salt should be added to the flour to enhance the flavour of the pastry.

Types of Pastry

There are seven different types of pastry all made using the same basic ingredients. The methods by which these pastries are prepared and the combination of ingredients used vary. Similarly, the techniques observed in handling and the storage of the pastry vary accordingly and these are explained in the basic recipes at the beginning of each chapter. The recipes also give a guide to the finished quantity of the made-up pastry.

Shortcrust Pastry This pastry is a mixture of plain flour and fat (usually margarine or butter) normally used in the ratio of half fat to flour. The fat is rubbed into the flour and the mixture moistened with water. The pastry may be enriched by the addition of extra fat, sugar or the substitution of egg yolk for the water.
Uses: Both sweet and savoury. Pies, tarts, flans and pasties.

Flaky, Puff and Rough Puff Pastries Puff pastry uses equal quantities of fat to plain flour while flaky and rough puff use three-quarters fat to plain flour. The use of strong flour strengthens the layers and increases the rise of the pastry. The fat is incorporated partly by rubbing in and partly by rolling into the dough. It is necessary to keep the pastry well chilled during the rolling process.
Uses: Both sweet and savoury. Pies, vol-au-vent, mille feuilles, turnovers and cocktail bits.

Suet Crust Pastry This pastry uses shredded suet and self-raising flour in the ratio of half fat to flour. It is mixed to a soft dough with water.

Uses: Both sweet and savoury. Steamed or baked puddings, roly-polys, dumplings and pizza bases.

Hot Water Crust Pastry Here plain flour is mixed with a boiling mixture of water, milk and lard in the ratio one-third fat to flour. *Uses:* This pastry is not ideally suited to sweet dishes and is therefore used for savoury pies and pasties.

Choux Pastry Butter or margarine is melted with water and brought to the boil. Plain flour is added and eggs are beaten into the slightly cooled mixture to form a glossy paste.
Uses: Both sweet and savoury. Profiteroles, buns, éclairs, gâteaux and as a topping for casseroles.

Working with Pastry

Lightness in handling and, for most pastry, cool ingredients and utensils are all part of the secret of success. When mixing short-crust pastry avoid using too much water and when rolling out the pastry do not use too much flour. Keep the surface clean and evenly floured and flour the rolling pin lightly. Work lightly, do not press heavily on the rolling pin and roll in one direction turning the pastry slightly to keep an even thickness. Do not turn the pastry over during rolling and do not stretch the pastry as this will cause it to shrink during cooking. Roll the pastry out to as near the required size as possible in order to avoid wastage. To lift pastry from a work surface on to a dish, roll it loosely over a lightly-floured rolling pin. Lift it over the dish and unroll it carefully in the required position. If possible, pastry dishes should be chilled after rolling and before cooking.

Bake 'blind' This is the term used when a pastry case is par-cooked before the filling is added. The empty pastry shell will bubble up unless it is covered and weighted down slightly. Place a piece of greaseproof paper over the pastry and sprinkle over a few dried peas or beans. Bake according to the recipe. Alternatively, aluminium cooking foil may be used with the shiny side facing upwards. Since the foil reflects the heat and is fairly rigid, it will prevent the pastry from rising so there is no need to use baking beans.

'Knock-up' This is a method of sealing pastry edges. Where two edges of pastry are to be sealed, lightly dampen one with water then press both firmly together. Pressing lightly on the edge of the pastry and using the side of the index finger, use the wrong side of a round-bladed knife to gently knock the edge of the pastry and seal the edge. This 'knocking-up' process is particularly useful for pies and tarts.

Decoration The method and type of decoration depends on the type of pastry, the size and shape of the dish, whether it is sweet or savoury and the occasion for which it is being served. The sealed edges should be neatly finished by pinching together using the thumb and forefinger, if the pastry is twisted at the same time as pinching, a different effect will be achieved. To make a scalloped edge, press the pastry outwards and, at the same time use the blunt edge of a knife to pull the pastry next to the finger inwards thus forming a scallop. The scallops may be large or small depending on the size of the item and whether it is sweet or savoury – sweet dishes look more attractive with small neat edging. Other methods of decoration to be used on the edges of pastry include pressing lightly with a fork or the addition of twisted or plaited strips of pastry which may be attached to the edge by dampening slightly.

The top of the dish may be decorated with cut-out shapes – small circles of pastry, heart shapes or stars for example, or larger shapes resembling apples, pears or fish. One of the easiest ways of finishing off a pastry dish is by cutting out pastry leaves and marking their veins lightly with a pointed knife. Dampen these and place on the pastry. Small balls of pastry can also look attractive if used carefully. Hot water crust pastry may be moulded into leaves or balls or may be used to produce a flower effect. The possibilities are endless and are quite open to the imagination of the cook. History has seen the making of many an elaborately-sculptured pastry creation which would be far beyond the palate or interest of most cooks but certainly proves the versatility of this basic mixture.

Glazing Many pastry dishes require glazing before they are cooked. Savoury dishes look very tempting when glazed with a little beaten egg. Sweet dishes are best with a weaker glaze and therefore a little milk is more suitable. Sugar may be sprinkled over sweet dishes before cooking to give a slightly crunchy top. The glaze should always be even and light. It is a good idea to check that the glaze is even during cooking and to brush lightly with a little more if necessary.

To Line a Flan Tin Many recipes require a pastry flan case. The flan may be made in a flan dish or loose-bottomed flan tin. The pastry should be rolled out to approximately 3.5–5 cm/$1\frac{1}{2}$–2 inches larger than the diameter of the tin. Lift the pastry carefully rolling it over a lightly-floured rolling pin. Place in position over the tin and unroll. Carefully lift the edge of the pastry with one hand and press into the base and sides of the tin with the other. Trim any excess pastry by rolling the rolling pin over the top of the dish or tin.

To Prepare a Pie Dish A pie is a dish which has a filling and a lid but no pastry base. The dish should be prepared by lining the rim with pastry so that the lid has an edge which may be sealed. Roll out the pastry to 5 cm/2 inches larger than the top of the dish and cut a 2.5-cm/1-inch strip from the edge. Press this strip of pastry on to the dampened rim of the dish. Add the filling to the dish. Dampen the pastry rim and place the lid on top. Seal the edges together and decorate and glaze the pie.

Caraway Cheese Biscuits (see page 28); Savoury Pinwheels (see page 64); Savoury Tartlets (see page 31); Banana Bacon Savouries (see page 62).

CHAPTER 2

Shortcrust Pastry

Shortcrust pastry should be crisp and short with a fine, even texture. For this reason the pastry should be handled quickly and lightly using chilled ingredients. Chilling the pastry item before cooking helps to make the finished result short in texture. This recipe produces enough pastry to line a 23-cm/9-inch flan tin or make 20–24 tartlets and is referred to as 'I quantity' throughout this chapter.

225 g/8 oz plain flour
pinch of salt
100 g/4 oz margarine
2 tablespoons cold water

Place the flour and salt in a bowl. Add the margarine and rub in lightly with the fingertips until the mixture resembles fine bread-crumbs. Sprinkle over the water and mix, using a round-bladed knife, until the mixture begins to bind together to form a dough. Knead together very lightly and use as required.

One-stage method

For quickness, the pastry may be combined using an electric food mixer. Place the flour and salt in a bowl, add the margarine in small pieces and sprinkle over the water. Mix using an electric mixer on the slowest speed, gradually increasing the speed as the mixture binds together. Knead lightly to form a dough and use as required.

Apple and Banana Pie (see page 37); Pepper and Chicken Pie (see page 21).

Sweet Flan Pastry

225 g/8 oz plain flour
pinch of salt
175 g/6 oz butter
50 g/2 oz castor sugar
1 egg yolk

Place the flour and salt in a bowl. Rub in the butter with the finger-tips until the mixture resembles fine breadcrumbs. Add the castor sugar and egg yolk. Mix, using a round-bladed knife, until the mixture binds together to form a dough. Knead lightly and use as required.

Wholewheat Pastry

175 g/6 oz plain wholewheat flour
50 g/2 oz plain flour
generous pinch of salt
100 g/4 oz margarine
3 tablespoons water

Follow the method for Shortcrust pastry (see page 19) and use as required.

Sweet Wholewheat Pastry

175 g/6 oz plain wholewheat flour
50 g/2 oz plain flour
175 g/6 oz butter
25 g/1 oz light soft brown sugar
1 egg yolk

Follow the method for Sweet flan pastry (see above) and use as required.

Pepper and Chicken Pie

(Illustrated on page 18)
1 quantity Shortcrust pastry (see page 19)
450 g/1 lb uncooked chicken meat
25 g/1 oz butter
1 large onion, chopped
2 red peppers, seeded and sliced
100 g/4 oz button mushrooms, halved
salt and freshly ground black pepper
2 tablespoons plain flour
150 ml/$\frac{1}{4}$ pint chicken stock
150 ml/$\frac{1}{4}$ pint dry vermouth
150 ml/$\frac{1}{4}$ pint double cream
beaten egg or milk to glaze

Make the pastry according to the recipe instructions. Cut the chicken into bite-sized pieces. Melt the butter in a saucepan, add the chicken, onion and pepper and cook until lightly browned. Add the mushrooms and season generously then stir in the flour. Gradually add the chicken stock and bring to the boil. Stir in the vermouth, remove from the heat and stir in the cream. Allow to cool.

Roll out the pastry to approximately 3.5 cm/1$\frac{1}{2}$ inches larger than a 1.15-litre/2-pint pie dish. Trim a strip of pastry from the edge to line the dampened rim of the pie dish. Turn the chicken mixture into the dish. Dampen the pastry rim with water and cover with the pastry lid. Seal the edges and use any pastry trimmings to decorate the pie. Brush with a little beaten egg or milk and bake in a moderately hot oven (200°C, 400°F, Gas Mark 6) for 40 minutes until golden brown. Serve immediately. *Serves 4–6*

Lemon Fish Pie

(Illustrated on page 72)
1 quantity Shortcrust pastry (see page 19)
grated rind of 3 lemons
50 g/2 oz butter
1 onion, chopped
1 tablespoon plain flour
300 ml/½ pint milk
2 tablespoons chopped parsley
100 g/4 oz peeled prawns
450 g/1 lb cooked white fish (for example cod,
haddock or coley)
salt and freshly ground black pepper
beaten egg or milk to glaze

Make the pastry according to the recipe instructions adding the grated rind of two of the lemons to the flour. Roll a little of the pastry into a piece long enough to line the rim of a 1.15-litre/2-pint pie dish. Dampen the edge of the dish with water and line with the pastry.

Melt the butter in a saucepan, add the onion and cook until soft but not browned. Stir in the flour and cook for a few minutes. Gradually stir in the milk and bring to the boil, stirring continuously. Add the parsley, prawns and remaining lemon rind. Remove any skin and bones from the fish, flake roughly and place in the pie dish. Season the sauce to taste and pour over the fish.

Roll out the remaining pastry to fit the top of the dish. Dampen the pastry rim with water and place the pastry lid on the pie. Seal the edges and use any pastry trimmings to decorate the top. Make a small hole in the pie to allow any steam to escape during cooking. Brush with a little beaten egg or milk and bake in a moderately hot oven (190°C, 375°F, Gas Mark 5) for 30–40 minutes until golden. *Serves 4*

Cornish Pasties

1 quantity Shortcrust pastry (see page 19)
225 g/8 oz braising steak
1 carrot
1 medium potato
1 medium onion, chopped
2 tablespoons beef stock
salt and freshly ground black pepper
2 tablespoons chopped parsley
beaten egg or milk to glaze

Grease a baking tray. Make the pastry according to the recipe instructions. Cut the meat into small cubes and dice the carrot and potato. Mix the meat and vegetables with the stock and season generously. Stir in the chopped parsley.

Divide the pastry into four pieces and roll each piece out to a 15-cm/6-inch circle. Divide the meat mixture between the pastry circles and dampen the edges with water. Bring the edges together over the middle of the filling and seal to form an enclosed pasty. Place on the baking tray and brush with a little beaten egg or milk then bake in a moderately hot oven (200°C, 400°F, Gas Mark 6) for 15 minutes. Reduce the temperature to moderate (180°C, 350°F, Gas Mark 4) and cook for a further 50–60 minutes. Serve hot or cold. *Makes 4*

Pork and Prune Pasties

I quantity Shortcrust pastry (see page 19)
350 g/12 oz lean pork
I onion, chopped
$\frac{1}{2}$ teaspoon chopped fresh sage
salt and freshly ground black pepper
100 g/4 oz prunes
2 tablespoons dry cider or chicken stock
beaten egg or milk to glaze

Grease a baking tray. Make the pastry according to the recipe instructions. Cut the pork into small cubes and mix with the onion, sage and seasoning to taste. Cut the prune flesh away from the stones and roughly chop. Mix with the meat and cider or chicken stock.

Divide the pastry into four pieces and roll each piece out to a 15-cm/6-inch circle. Divide the meat mixture between the circles, dampen the edges with water and bring together over the middle of the filling. Seal the edges and place the pasties on the baking tray. Brush with a little beaten egg or milk and bake in a moderately hot oven (200°C, 400°F, Gas Mark 6) for 15 minutes then reduce the oven temperature to moderate (180°C, 350°F, Gas Mark 4) and bake for a further 50–60 minutes. Serve hot. *Makes 4*

Layered Vegetable Pie

(Illustrated on page 92)
1 quantity Shortcrust pastry (see page 19)
50 g/2 oz mature Cheddar cheese, finely grated
2 large potatoes
4 carrots
2 large onions
225 g/8 oz button mushrooms
salt and freshly ground black pepper
25 g/1 oz butter
1 tablespoon plain flour
300 ml/$\frac{1}{2}$ pint milk
25 g/1 oz mature Cheddar cheese, finely grated
50 g/2 oz butter
2 tablespoons chopped parsley
beaten egg or milk to glaze

Make the pastry according to the recipe instructions adding the 50 g/2 oz grated cheese to the rubbed-in ingredients before mixing in the water. Roll out to approximately 3.5 cm/1$\frac{1}{2}$ inches larger than a 1.75-litre/3-pint pie dish. Trim a strip of pastry from the edge to line the rim of the pie dish.

Par-boil the potatoes, carrots and onions for 10 minutes then slice fairly thickly. Layer the vegetables and mushrooms in the dish, seasoning generously between each layer.

Melt the 25 g/1 oz butter in a saucepan, stir in the flour and gradually add the milk. Season and stir in the 25 g/1 oz cheese, the remaining butter and parsley. Carefully pour the sauce over the vegetables, encouraging it to run down between the layers.

Dampen the rim of the dish with water and cover with the pastry strip. Dampen the pastry strip with water and top with the pastry lid. Seal the edges and use any trimmings to decorate the pie. Brush with a little beaten egg or milk and bake in a moderate oven (180°C, 350°F, Gas Mark 4) for 1 hour. The pie should be golden brown and the vegetables cooked through. *Serves 4–6*

Chicken and Gammon Pie

I quantity Shortcrust pastry (see page 19)
25 g/I oz butter
2 large onions, sliced
350 g/12 oz uncooked chicken meat
4 gammon steaks, rinds removed
2 tablespoons redcurrant jelly
150 ml/¼ pint dry red wine
grated rind and juice of I large orange
freshly ground black pepper
beaten egg or milk to glaze

Make the pastry according to the recipe instructions. Melt the butter in a large pan, add the onion and sauté until soft but not browned. Place the chicken between two pieces of dampened greaseproof paper and beat out as thinly as possible. Similarly, beat out the gammon.

Roll out the pastry to approximately 3.5 cm/1½ inches larger than a 1.15-litre/2-pint pie dish. Trim a strip of pastry from the edge to line the rim of the pie dish. Layer the meats with the onion in the dish. To make the sauce, place the redcurrant jelly, wine, orange rind and juice in a saucepan and heat gently until dissolved and well mixed. Season with a little freshly ground black pepper and pour over the meats.

Dampen the rim of the dish with water and cover with the pastry strip. Dampen the pastry strip with water and top with the pastry lid. Seal the edges and use any pastry trimmings to decorate the pie. Brush with a little beaten egg or milk and bake in a moderate oven (180°C, 350°F, Gas Mark 4) for I hour. The pie should be golden brown and thoroughly cooked. Serve hot or cold. *Serves 4*

Cheesy Sausage Plait

1 quantity Shortcrust pastry (see page 19)
25 g/1 oz butter
1 large onion, chopped
salt and freshly ground black pepper
4 tablespoons fresh breadcrumbs
2 teaspoons wholegrain mustard
350 g/12 oz sausagemeat
100 g/4 oz Sage Derby cheese, grated
beaten egg or milk to glaze

Make the pastry according to the recipe instructions. Roll out the pastry to give an oblong measuring 23 × 30 cm/9 × 12 inches.

Melt the butter, add the onion and cook until soft but not browned. Season generously then stir in the breadcrumbs, mustard, sausagemeat and cheese. Mix until thoroughly combined.

Arrange the filling down the middle of the pastry. Cut the edges of the pastry diagonally into 2.5-cm/1-inch strips. Fold these strips of pastry over the filling, dampening the edges with water in order to hold them in place, to form a plait. Brush with a little beaten egg or milk and bake in a moderately hot oven (190°C, 375°F, Gas Mark 5) for 40–45 minutes. Serve warm. *Serves 4–6*

Caraway Cheese Biscuits

(Illustrated on page 17)
These little biscuits are ideal for serving at parties or with drinks. They will freeze well without the cream cheese decoration.

I quantity Shortcrust pastry (see page 19)
100 g/4 oz mature Cheddar cheese, finely grated
I teaspoon dry mustard
2 teaspoons caraway seeds
beaten egg or milk to glaze
100 g/4 oz cream cheese
50 g/2 oz stuffed green olives, thickly sliced

Grease two baking trays. Make the pastry according to the recipe instructions, adding the grated cheese, mustard and caraway seeds to the rubbed-in dry ingredients. Stir well, add the pastry water and roll out to 5 mm/$\frac{1}{4}$ inch thickness. Use a 3.5-cm/$1\frac{1}{2}$-inch pastry cutter to cut out the biscuits. Place on the baking trays, brush with a little beaten egg or milk and bake in a moderately hot oven (200°C, 400°F, Gas Mark 6) for 10–15 minutes. Cool on a wire rack.

Fit a piping bag with a small star nozzle and fill with the cream cheese. Pipe a little cream cheese on top of each biscuit and top with a slice of olive. *Makes 35*

Samosas with Yogurt Dressing

(Illustrated on page 91)
These little deep-fried pasties are a traditional Indian snack,
usually made from mixed vegetables with spices added.

175 g/6 oz minced lamb
1 small onion, finely chopped
1 teaspoon ground cumin
1 teaspoon ground coriander
$\frac{1}{4}$ teaspoon mustard seeds (optional)
1 tablespoon grated root ginger
1 large clove garlic, crushed
salt and freshly ground black pepper
1 small carrot, par-boiled and diced
1 small potato, par-boiled and diced
50 g/2 oz frozen peas
1 quantity Shortcrust pastry (see page 19)
1 egg, lightly beaten
oil for deep frying
150 ml/$\frac{1}{4}$ pint natural yogurt

Place the lamb in a frying pan with the onion and cook gently until the fat runs. Add the cumin, coriander, mustard seeds if used, ginger and garlic and continue to cook until the onion is soft. Season generously then stir in the vegetables.

Make the pastry according to the recipe instructions, mixing the dry ingredients together with the egg as well as the water to form a soft dough. Knead lightly until smooth then divide into 12 equal portions. Roll each piece of dough out to give a 10-cm/4-inch square. Place some of the filling on the pastry and dampen the edges with water. Fold two opposite corners together and seal the edges to form a triangular pasty.

Deep fry the samosas, a few at a time, until golden brown, about 3–5 minutes. Drain on absorbent kitchen paper and serve hot with a little natural yogurt. *Makes 12*

Winter Pie

This is a wholesome family pie which is ideal for cold winter days when appetites are running high!

1 quantity Wholewheat pastry (see page 20)
225 g/8 oz minced beef
225 g/8 oz minced pork
1 egg, lightly beaten
salt and freshly ground black pepper
2 tablespoons cooking oil
1 large leek, thinly sliced
2 carrots, thinly sliced
1 teaspoon powdered sage
1 tablespoon plain flour
300 ml/½ pint beef stock
beaten egg or milk to glaze

Make the pastry according to the recipe instructions and roll out slightly larger than the top of a 1.15-litre/2-pint pie dish. Trim a strip of pastry from the edge and use to line the dampened rim of the pie dish.

Mix the minced meats with the egg and season generously. Roll into small, bite-sized meatballs using wet hands. Heat the oil and quickly fry the meatballs until brown on all sides. Remove and drain on absorbent kitchen paper. Quickly sauté the leek with the carrot and sage for a minute then stir in the flour and add the stock. Return the meatballs to the sauce and arrange the filling in the pie, piling the meatballs slightly in the middle. Dampen the pastry rim with water. Top with the pastry lid and use any trimmings to decorate the pie. Brush with beaten egg or milk and bake in a moderately hot oven (200°C, 400°F, Gas Mark 6) for 15 minutes then reduce the temperature to moderate (180°C, 350°F, Gas Mark 4) and cook for a further 30–35 minutes. Serve immediately. *Serves 4*

Savoury Tartlets

(Illustrated on page 17)
1 quantity Shortcrust pastry (see page 19)
350 g/12 oz cream cheese
salt and freshly ground black pepper
2 teaspoons wholegrain mustard
1 teaspoon chopped chives
Toppings:
6 slices smoked salmon
6 slices Parma ham
6 rashers lean bacon, rinds removed
6 stuffed green olives
6 canned pineapple chunks, drained
6 black olives
6 whole almonds, shelled

Make the pastry according to the recipe instructions. Roll out 20–24 (7.5-cm/3-inch) rounds and use to line patty tins. Alternatively, using boat-shaped tins as a guide, cut out pieces of pastry approximately 5–10 mm/$\frac{1}{4}$–$\frac{1}{2}$ inch larger than the tins and make pastry boats. Prick the lined tins all over and chill for 20 minutes. Bake in a moderately hot oven (200°C, 400°F, Gas Mark 6) for 8–12 minutes until lightly browned and cooked. Cool on a wire rack.

Lightly beat the cream cheese with a little seasoning, the mustard and chives. Spoon or pipe the filling into the tartlets or boats. Roll the salmon and ham and use to top half of the tartlets. Roll the bacon, place on metal skewers and cook under a hot grill until crisp. Drain and cool on absorbent kitchen paper. Place a stuffed olive, bacon roll and pineapple chunk on each of six cocktail sticks and place one on each of six of the tartlets. Stone the black olives and place an almond in the cavity. Place one of these on each of the remaining tartlets. Serve on a large platter.

Alternatively, all the tartlets may be topped with one topping in which case the quantities of the chosen topping should be increased accordingly. *Makes 20–24*

Quiche Lorraine

(Illustrated on pages 102–3)
Quiche also tastes delicious when the pastry case is
made using wholewheat pastry.

1 quantity Shortcrust pastry (see page 19)
50 g/2 oz butter
1 large onion, finely chopped
3 eggs
300 ml/½ pint single cream or milk
salt and freshly ground black pepper
225 g/8 oz streaky bacon, rind removed and
coarsely chopped
100 g/4 oz Gruyère cheese, thinly sliced
2 teaspoons chopped mixed fresh herbs
Garnish
2 tomatoes, sliced
sprigs of parsley

Make the pastry according to the recipe instructions and use to line a 23-cm/9-inch flan tin. Bake the flan 'blind' (see page 14) in a moderately hot oven (200°C, 400°F, Gas Mark 6) for 15 minutes, then remove the foil or beans and continue to cook for a further 5 minutes.

Meanwhile prepare the filling. Melt the butter in a frying pan, add the onion and cook until the onion is soft but not browned. Beat the eggs together and stir in the cream or milk. Season well. Place the onion and bacon in the bottom of the flan and arrange the Gruyère and herbs on top. Pour over the egg and cream mixture and bake in a moderate oven (180°C, 350°F, Gas Mark 4) for 35–40 minutes until set and golden brown. Garnish with sliced tomatoes and a few sprigs of parsley. *Serves 4–6*

Variations
Herby Mushroom Quiche: Add 2 tablespoons chopped fresh mixed herbs to the pastry before mixing in the water. Omit the bacon, place the cooked onion in the bottom of the quiche and top with 100 g/4 oz halved button mushrooms. Continue as above.

Pepper Quiche: Substitute I small red and I small green pepper, seeded and finely chopped, for the bacon and Gruyère. Continue as above.

Spinach Quiche: Substitute I (225-g/8-oz) packet chopped frozen spinach for the bacon, and use 100 g/4 oz grated Cheddar cheese instead of the Gruyère. Beat I teaspoon ground nutmeg into the eggs. Continue as above.

Blue Cheese Quiche: Substitute 175 g/6 oz blue cheese for the onion, bacon and Gruyère. Crumble the blue cheese into the flan and continue as above.

Cream Cheese and Ham Flan

I quantity Shortcrust pastry (see page 19)
50 g/2 oz Cheddar cheese, finely grated
25 g/I oz butter
I large onion, finely chopped
175 g/6 oz cooked ham, chopped
100 g/4 oz button mushrooms, sliced
175 g/6 oz full-fat soft cheese
I egg
salt and freshly ground black pepper

Make the pastry according to the recipe instructions, adding the grated cheese to the dry, rubbed-in ingredients. Use to line a 23-cm/9-inch loose-bottomed flan tin or dish. Bake 'blind' (see page 14) in a moderately hot oven (200°C, 400°F, Gas Mark 6) for 20 minutes.

Melt the butter in a small frying pan, add the onion and cook until soft but not browned. Stir in the ham and mushrooms and cool slightly. Beat the soft cheese and egg together, season to taste and mix in the onion mixture. Spread over the flan case and bake in a moderate oven (180°C, 350°F, Gas Mark 4) for 30–40 minutes until lightly browned and set. Serve warm or cold. *Serves 6*

Spinach Burgers in Pastry

I quantity Wholewheat pastry (see page 20)
50 g/2 oz butter
I large onion, finely chopped
I clove garlic, crushed
2 (225-g/8-oz) packets chopped spinach, well drained
100 g/4 oz Cheddar cheese, finely grated
4 tablespoons fresh breadcrumbs
salt and freshly ground black pepper
I egg, beaten
a few sesame seeds
beaten egg or milk to glaze

Make the pastry according to the recipe instructions and divide
into eight portions. Roll out each portion to give two 8.5-cm/3½-
inch rounds.

To prepare the filling, melt the butter in a frying pan and gently
sauté the onion and garlic until soft but not browned. Add the onion
and garlic to the spinach, cheese and breadcrumbs. Mix well and
season to taste. Add enough egg to bind the mixture together and
divide into eight portions. Shape each portion into a 7.5-cm/3-inch
round and place on to one of the pastry rounds. Dampen the edges
of the pastry with water and place another round on top, sealing
and pinching the edges together. Snip the top of the pastry with
scissors, brush with beaten egg or milk and sprinkle with sesame
seeds. Repeat with the other pastry portions, place on a baking tray
and cook in a moderately hot oven (200°C, 400°F, Gas Mark 6) for
30 minutes. *Makes 8*

Plum and Banana Pie (see page 37); Savoury Mince Gougère (see page 111);
Apricot Horns (see page 79).

Rhubarb and Banana Pie

450 g/1 lb fresh or frozen rhubarb, sliced
grated rind and juice of 1 large orange
100 g/4 oz light soft brown sugar
2 bananas, sliced
1 quantity Shortcrust pastry (see page 19)
milk to glaze

Mix the rhubarb with the orange rind and juice, sugar and bananas. Place in a 1.15-litre/2-pint pie dish.

Make the pastry according to the recipe instructions and roll out to approximately 3.5 cm/1½ inches larger than the pie dish. Cut a strip from the edge of the pastry and use to line the dampened rim of the dish. Dampen the pastry rim with water and cover with the lid. Trim, seal and flute the edges. Use any pastry trimmings to decorate the pie. Brush with a little milk and bake in a moderately hot oven (190°C, 375°F, Gas Mark 5) for 1–1¼ hours. Serve hot with clotted cream. *Serves 6*

Variations

Plum and Banana Pie: (*Illustrated on page 35*) Substitute 450 g/1 lb halved and stoned plums for the rhubarb and cook as above.

Apricot and Raspberry Pie: (*Illustrated on jacket*) Substitute 450 g/ 1 lb skinned and halved apricots and 225 g/8 oz raspberries for the rhubarb and bananas and cook as above.

Apple and Banana Pie: (*Illustrated on page 18*) Substitute 450 g/1 lb peeled, cored and sliced apples for the rhubarb and cook as above.

Cider Apple Flan (see page 47); Mandarin Flan (see page 47); Strawberry Flan (see page 47).

Baked Cheesecake

I quantity Sweet flan pastry (see page 20)
225 g/8 oz cream cheese
grated rind and juice of I lemon
75 g/3 oz castor sugar
I egg, separated
2 tablespoons self-raising flour
150 ml/¼ pint double cream
75 g/3 oz raisins

Make the pastry according to the recipe instructions and use to line a 23-cm/9-inch flan tin. Bake the flan 'blind' (see page 14) in a moderately hot oven (200°C, 400°F, Gas Mark 6) for 15 minutes, remove the foil or baking beans and continue to cook for a further 5 minutes.

Meanwhile prepare the filling. Mix together the cream cheese, rind and juice of the lemon, castor sugar, egg yolk, flour and cream. Whisk the egg white until stiff and carefully fold into the creamed ingredients together with the raisins. Place in the flan case and bake in a moderate oven (180°C, 350°F, Gas Mark 4) for 45 minutes. Cool and serve lightly chilled. *Serves 8*

Strawberry and Orange Chiffon Pie

1 quantity Sweet flan pastry (see page 20)
100 g/4 oz castor sugar
2 eggs, separated
450 g/1 lb fresh or frozen strawberries
grated rind of 2 oranges
juice of 1 orange
15 g/½ oz powdered gelatine
3 tablespoons hot water
150 ml/¼ pint double cream, lightly whipped

Make the pastry according to the recipe instructions and use to line a 25-cm/10-inch flan tin. Bake the flan 'blind' (see page 14) in a moderately hot oven (200°C, 400°F, Gas Mark 6) for 15 minutes, remove the foil or baking beans and continue to cook for a further 15–20 minutes or until cooked. Cool.

Meanwhile prepare the filling. Whisk the sugar and egg yolks together until thick and creamy. Reserve a quarter of the strawberries for decoration and reduce the remainder in a liquidiser or by passing through a fine sieve to a purée. Add the purée together with the orange rind and juice to the creamed yolks. Dissolve the gelatine in the hot water in a basin over boiling water. Stir the gelatine into the egg mixture and leave until half set. Whisk the egg whites until stiff. Lightly fold the cream into the filling, and finally fold in the egg whites. Swirl into the pastry case and leave to set. Decorate with the reserved strawberries and serve chilled. *Serves 6–8*

Coconut Cream Pie

1 quantity Sweet flan pastry (see page 20)
1 coconut
25 g/1 oz cornflour
50 g/2 oz castor sugar
150 ml/¼ pint milk
2 egg yolks
150 ml/¼ pint coconut milk
300 ml/½ pint double cream
Topping
75 g/3 oz soft brown sugar

Make the pastry according to the recipe instructions and use to line a 23-cm/9-inch flan tin. Bake the flan 'blind' (see page 14) in a moderate oven (180°C, 350°F, Gas Mark 4) for 20 minutes and then remove the cooking foil or baking beans and cook for a further 20–30 minutes until golden brown. Cool.

Meanwhile prepare the filling. Finely mince the coconut flesh or reduce as finely as possible in a food processor or liquidiser. Mix the cornflour with the sugar, milk, egg yolks and coconut milk until smooth. Heat, stirring continuously, until the custard thickens. Remove from the heat, stir in the double cream and coconut flesh and pour into the flan case. Chill thoroughly.

Sprinkle the brown sugar on top of the flan and grill until the sugar melts and bubbles. Serve immediately. *Serves 6–8*

Apple and Raisin Plate Tart

1 quantity Shortcrust pastry (see page 19)
grated rind of 1 large orange
2 tablespoons rum (optional)
50 g/2 oz raisins
450 g/1 lb cooking apples, peeled, cored and sliced
50 g/2 oz castor sugar

Make the pastry according to the recipe instructions, adding the orange rind after rubbing in the dry ingredients. Divide the pastry in half, and use one half to line an 18-cm/7-inch pie plate. Warm the rum, if used, and soak the raisins in it for 2 hours. Alternatively, use the raisins unsoaked.

Layer the apple, sugar and raisins on the pie plate. Dampen the pastry rim with water and cover with the remaining pastry lid. Seal and flute the edges. Bake in a moderately hot oven (200°C, 400°F, Gas Mark 6) for 15 minutes and then reduce the temperature to moderate (180°C, 350°F, Gas Mark 4) and cook for a further 40 minutes. Serves 4

Raspberry and Apple Layer

(Illustrated on page 53)
1 quantity Sweet flan pastry (see page 20)
100 g/4 oz hazelnuts, chopped
450 g/1 lb cooking apples, peeled, cored and sliced
100 g/4 oz castor sugar
100 g/4 oz fresh or frozen raspberries
100 g/4 oz full-fat soft cheese
2 tablespoons clear honey
150 ml/¼ pint double cream

Make the pastry according to the recipe instructions, adding 75 g/3 oz of the chopped hazelnuts to the rubbed-in ingredients before adding the egg. Divide the pastry in half and roll out to give two 18-cm/7-inch rounds. Trim the edges of the rounds and chill in the refrigerator for 30 minutes. Sprinkle the top of one round with the remaining nuts. Place on a baking tray and bake in a moderately hot oven (200°C, 400°F, Gas Mark 6) for 20 minutes. Cool on a wire rack.

Meanwhile prepare the filling. Cook the apples with the sugar until just soft and add to the raspberries. Leave until cool. Stir the cheese and honey together until well mixed. Whip the cream until stiff and add to the cheese mixture. Spread this cream mixture over the pastry round without the nuts on top. Then top with the apple and raspberry mixture and finally cover with the second round of pastry topped with the chopped nuts. Chill and serve. *Serves 4*

Star Mincemeat Flan

$1\frac{1}{2}$ quantities Sweet flan pastry (see page 20)
grated rind of 1 orange
450 g/1 lb mincemeat
2 tablespoons rum or brandy
milk to glaze

Make the pastry according to the recipe instructions, adding the orange rind to the dry ingredients before mixing in the egg yolk. Reserve one-third of the pastry and use the remainder to line a 23-cm/9-inch flan tin. Bake the flan 'blind' (see page 14) in a moderately hot oven (200°C, 400°F, Gas Mark 6) for 15 minutes. Remove from the oven and spread the mincemeat over the flan. Sprinkle the rum or brandy over the filling.

Roll out the remaining pastry to 5 mm/$\frac{1}{4}$ inch thickness and cut out 16 stars using a star-shaped pastry cutter. Place these stars around the edge of the flan, overlapping them slightly. Brush with milk and cook in a moderate oven (180°C, 350°F, Gas Mark 4) for 30–40 minutes. *Serves 8*

Baked Alaska Flan

(Illustrated on page 53)
1 quantity Sweet flan pastry (see page 20)
1 egg, separated
50 g/2 oz castor sugar
6 peaches, peeled and stoned
150 ml/¼ pint double cream, lightly whipped
225 g/8 oz fresh or frozen raspberries
Meringue
3 egg whites
175 g/6 oz castor sugar

Make the pastry according to the recipe instructions and use to line a 23-cm/9-inch flan tin. Prick the pastry all over and bake 'blind' (see page 14) for 15 minutes in a moderately hot oven (200°C, 400°F, Gas Mark 6). Remove the foil or baking beans and cook for a further 15 minutes until browned and cooked.

Meanwhile prepare the ice cream. Whisk the egg yolk with the sugar until pale and creamy. In a liquidiser, blend four of the peaches to a smooth purée and stir into the yolk mixture together with the whipped cream. Transfer to a shallow freezer container and place in a freezer or the freezing compartment of the refrigerator until half frozen. Whisk thoroughly to form an even 'sludge'. Whisk the reserved egg white until stiff and fold into the ice cream. Return to the freezer and freeze until firm.

Whisk the egg whites for the meringue until stiff. Whisk the castor sugar vigorously into the whites (preferably using an electric whisk) until very stiff and very glossy. Slice the remaining peaches and place in the cooled flan case. Spoon the ice cream over the top, cover with the raspberries and quickly swirl the meringue over to completely cover the ice cream and the edges of the flan. Bake in a very hot oven (240°C, 475°F, Gas Mark 9) for 1–2 minutes until the top of the meringue tinges brown then serve immediately. *Serves 6–8*

Brandied Pear Cheesecake

I quantity Sweet flan pastry (see page 20)
225 g/8 oz cream cheese
50 g/2 oz castor sugar
3 tablespoons rum
I egg, beaten
2 tablespoons plain flour
3 firm pears
juice of $\frac{1}{2}$ lemon
100 g/4 oz apricot jam, warmed and sieved

Make the pastry according to the recipe instructions and use to line a 23-cm/9-inch flan tin. Bake 'blind' (see page 14) in a moderately hot oven (200°C, 400°F, Gas Mark 6) for 15 minutes then remove the baking beans or cooking foil and cook for a further 5 minutes.

Meanwhile, beat the cream cheese with the sugar and rum. Gradually mix in the egg and plain flour and spread the mixture in the flan case. Peel and halve the pears. Remove their stalks and cores and brush all over with lemon juice. Arrange the pear halves on top of the flan and bake in a moderate oven (180°C, 350°F, Gas Mark 4) for 40–45 minutes or until the pears are soft. During cooking the pears may be brushed with any remaining lemon juice. Brush the top of the cheesecake with the warmed jam and leave until cold. Chill before serving. *Serves 6*

Honeyed Walnut Tart

I quantity Sweet wholewheat pastry (see page 20)
2 oranges
I lemon
225 g/8 oz walnut pieces
175 g/6 oz clear honey
I tablespoon Demerara sugar
150 ml/¼ pint double cream to decorate

Make the pastry according to the recipe instructions and use to line a 23-cm/9-inch flan tin. Bake 'blind' (see page 14) in a moderately hot oven (200°C, 400°F, Gas Mark 6) for 20 minutes.

Pare the rind from the oranges and lemon and cut into thin strips. Place in a saucepan, cover with water and bring to the boil then simmer for 15 minutes. Drain and mix with the walnuts, juice of half the lemon and the honey. Spread evenly over the flan case and sprinkle the sugar over the top. Bake in a moderately hot oven (200°C, 400°F, Gas Mark 6) for 10–15 minutes. Leave until just warm.

Whip the cream until stiff and pipe around the edge of the warm flan before serving. *Serves 6–8*

Somerset Plum Flan

1 quantity Sweet flan pastry (see page 20)
450 g/1 lb plums
100 g/4 oz sugar
300 ml/½ pint sweet cider

Make the pastry according to the recipe instructions and use to line a 23-cm/9-inch flan tin. Bake 'blind' (see page 14) in a moderate oven (180°C, 350°F, Gas Mark 4) for 20 minutes. Remove the baking beans or foil and cook for a further 20–25 minutes or until cooked and lightly browned. Leave until cool.

Halve the plums and remove the stones. Place the sugar and cider in a saucepan and stir over a low heat until dissolved. Add the plums and cook gently until just softened. Remove the plums with a slotted spoon and arrange in the flan case. Bring the cider syrup to the boil and cook until reduced by half. Cool slightly and pour over the plums. Serve with clotted cream. *Serves 6*

Variation

Cider Apple Flan: (*Illustrated on page 36*) Replace the plums with 450 g/1 lb sharp eating apples. Core and slice the apples, blanch them in the syrup for 1 minute then arrange in the flan case. Continue as above.

The cider glaze may also be used for soft fruit (for example strawberries) or canned fruit (for example mandarins). A little ground cinnamon gives an excellent flavour when the syrup is poured over mandarins. The flan case may be spread with a little sweetened, whipped cream before arranging the mandarins on top. (*Illustrated on page 36*).

CHAPTER 3

Flaky, Puff and Rough Puff Pastries

Flaky Pastry

Puff, flaky and rough puff pastries should be well-risen, light and crisp with distinct layers. The following recipes make approximately 675 g/1½ lb of pastry and are referred to as 'I quantity' throughout this chapter. It is essential to ensure that all ingredients are well chilled when making and rolling these pastries.

225 g/8 oz plain flour
generous pinch of salt
175 g/6 oz block margarine
7–8 tablespoons cold water

Place the flour and salt in a bowl. Divide the margarine into four portions and add one quarter to the flour. Rub in lightly until the mixture resembles very fine breadcrumbs.

Meanwhile thoroughly chill the remaining margarine. Mix the rubbed-in mixture with the water to form a soft dough. Knead lightly then roll out on a well-floured surface to give a rectangle measuring approximately 15 × 35 cm/6 × 14 inches. Mark the pastry into thirds and dot a quarter of the margarine over the top two-thirds leaving a small gap around the edges. Fold the bottom third over the middle third and the top third down over the bottom third to enclose the fat completely. Gently press the edges with a rolling pin to seal them. Give the pastry a quarter-turn in a clockwise direction so that the side edges are facing you. Carefully roll out the pastry to give a rectangle similar in size to the original piece of pastry. Dot another quarter of the margarine over the pastry and fold as before. Place on a well-floured plate and chill thoroughly in the refrigerator for 30 minutes or in the freezer for 10 minutes.

Roll and fold once more using the remaining margarine. Chill and roll and fold once more without any extra fat. Chill thoroughly before use.

Puff Pastry

225 g/8 oz block margarine
225 g/8 oz plain flour
generous pinch of salt
7–8 tablespoons cold water

Rub a quarter of the margarine into the flour and salt until the mixture resembles fine breadcrumbs. Form the remaining fat into a block measuring approximately 10 cm/4 inches square. Chill thoroughly in the refrigerator for 30 minutes, or in the freezer for 10 minutes.

Mix the rubbed-in ingredients with the water to form a soft dough. Knead lightly then roll out on a well-floured surface to give a rectangle measuring 15 × 35 cm/6 × 14 inches. Lightly mark the pastry into thirds and place the block of fat on the middle third. Fold the bottom third over the fat and fold the top third down over the bottom third to enclose the fat completely. Lightly press the side edges with a rolling pin to seal them.

Give the pastry a quarter-turn in a clockwise direction so that the side edges are now facing you. Lightly roll the pastry to form a rectangle similar in size to the original piece of pastry. Again, lightly mark the pastry into thirds and fold the bottom third over the middle third, then the top third down over the bottom third. Place on a well-floured plate and chill in the refrigerator for 30 minutes or in the freezer for 10 minutes. Roll out and fold the pastry as before to give a total number of six rollings. Chill the pastry between each rolling if the pastry becomes too warm to handle. Chill before use.

Rough Puff Pastry

Use similar quantities to those given on page 49 (Flaky pastry). Place the flour and salt in a bowl. Chill the margarine thoroughly and cut into chunks about the size of a walnut. Add the pieces of fat to the flour and toss to coat them thoroughly. Mix in the water to form a soft dough. Chill as before then roll and fold as for flaky pastry without using any extra fat. The pastry should be rolled four times.

Cheese and Apple Pie

$\frac{1}{2}$ quantity Puff pastry (see page 49)
50 g/2 oz butter
I large onion, finely chopped
450 g/I lb cooking apples, peeled, cored and sliced
225 g/8 oz bacon, rind removed and finely chopped
50 g/2 oz walnuts, coarsely chopped
225 g/8 oz Sage Derby cheese, sliced
salt and freshly ground black pepper
beaten egg or milk to glaze

Make the pastry according to the recipe instructions. Roll out slightly larger than the top of a 1.15-litre/2-pint pie dish. Cut a strip from the edge to line the dampened rim of the dish. Melt the butter in a frying pan, add the onion and apple and sauté for 5 minutes over a low heat. Layer the onion and apple mixture, bacon and walnuts with the cheese in the pie dish, seasoning each layer well. Dampen the pastry rim with water and cover with the pastry lid. Brush with beaten egg or milk and bake in a moderately hot oven (200°C, 400°F, Gas Mark 6) for 20–25 minutes. *Serves 4*

Chicken Parcels

I quantity Puff pastry (see page 49)
4 boned chicken breasts
4 tablespoons chopped fresh parsley and thyme
2 cloves garlic, crushed
2 tablespoons honey
I teaspoon lemon juice
salt and freshly ground black pepper
grated rind of I lemon
beaten egg or milk to glaze
Garnish
lemon twists
small bunches of watercress

Make the pastry according to the recipe instructions and divide into four pieces. Roll each piece out to a 15-cm/6-inch square.

Place the chicken breasts between two pieces of dampened greaseproof paper and beat out thinly. Mix the herbs, garlic, honey, lemon juice and seasoning together with the lemon rind. Divide between the chicken and fold the chicken over the filling. Place a piece of chicken on each piece of pastry, dampen the edges with water and fold the corners of the pastry over the chicken to meet in the middle like an envelope. Seal the edges and brush with beaten egg or milk. Place on a dampened baking tray and bake in a hot oven (220°C, 425°F, Gas Mark 7) for 15 minutes then reduce the temperature to moderate (180°C, 350°F, Gas Mark 4) and cook for a further 25–35 minutes. Serve garnished with twists of lemon and small bunches of watercress. *Makes 4*

Prawn Mille Feuilles

(Illustrated on page 72)
$\frac{1}{2}$ quantity Puff pastry (see page 49)
225 g/8 oz peeled prawns
75 g/3 oz smoked salmon pieces
3 spring onions, chopped
1 tablespoon lemon juice
2 tablespoons dry sherry
salt and freshly ground black pepper
150 ml/$\frac{1}{4}$ pint double cream
Garnish
few whole prawns
1 lemon, sliced
cucumber slices

Grease a baking tray. Make the pastry according to the recipe instructions and roll out to a 30-cm/12-inch square. Cut into three equal-sized oblong pieces and bake in a hot oven (230°C, 450°F, Gas Mark 8) for 10–15 minutes. Cool on a wire rack.

Mix the prawns, smoked salmon and spring onions together. Stir in the lemon juice and sherry with seasoning to taste. Whip the cream until just stiff. Stir in the prawn mixture and use to sandwich the puff pastry slices together. Place on a suitable serving dish and garnish with whole prawns, halved lemon slices and sliced cucumber. *Serves 4–6*

Baked Alaska Flan (see page 44); Raspberry and Apple Layer (see page 42); Stuffed Apple Dumplings (see page 90).

Camembert Puff

*This is an unusual and delicious lunch or supper dish. The
Camembert needs to be thoroughly chilled so that when
the pastry is cooked the cheese is just warm and very
runny.*

I whole ripe Camembert, weighing about 250 g/9 oz
$\frac{1}{4}$ quantity Puff pastry (see page 49)
beaten egg or milk to glaze

Scrape the rind off the Camembert and place in the freezer or the
freezing compartment of the refrigerator for $1\frac{1}{2}$ hours.
   Make the pastry according to the recipe instructions and roll out
to a 20-cm/8-inch square. Trim and dampen the edges with water.
Place the Camembert in the middle of the pastry and fold up the
corners to meet in the centre. Pinch the edges together to seal and
form an envelope shape. Brush with a little beaten egg or milk.
Place on a dampened baking tray and bake in a hot oven (230°C,
450°F, Gas Mark 8) for 10–15 minutes until golden and well puffed.
Serve immediately with a crisp salad. *Serves 4*

*Savoury Wrapped Pears (see page 68); Mushroom Puffs with Stilton Dressing
(see page 60).*

Stuffed Onions in Pastry

4 large onions
225 g/8 oz minced pork
100 g/4 oz bacon, rind removed and chopped
1 small red pepper, seeded and chopped
50 g/2 oz fresh breadcrumbs
2 tablespoons dry sherry or chicken stock
salt and freshly ground black pepper
$\frac{1}{2}$ teaspoon powdered sage
$\frac{1}{2}$ quantity Puff pastry (see page 49)
beaten egg or milk to glaze
Garnish
sprigs of parsley
tomato wedges

Cover the peeled whole onions with boiling water and simmer for 10 minutes. Drain and cool. Meanwhile gently cook the pork with the bacon and red pepper in a frying pan, stirring continuously until browned. Add the breadcrumbs and sherry or chicken stock and season to taste. Stir in the sage.

Carefully remove the inner rings from the onions leaving an empty shell. Finely chop the inner pieces and stir into the pork mixture. Use this mixture to firmly stuff the onion shells.

Make the pastry according to the recipe instructions and cut the pastry into four pieces. Roll each piece out to a 23-cm/9-inch round. Place an onion in the centre of each piece of pastry. Cut the surrounding pastry into strips, radiating out from the onion and carefully fold them over the onion. Dampen the edges of each strip with water and overlap the next to completely enclose the onion, trimming away any excess pastry which may gather at the top.

Place on a dampened baking tray and brush with a little beaten egg or milk. Bake in a moderately hot oven (200°C, 400°F, Gas Mark 6) for 30–35 minutes until puffed and golden. Serve garnished with sprigs of parsley and tomato wedges. *Serves 4*

Savoury Sausage Pie

½ quantity Puff pastry (see page 49)
50 g/2 oz butter
1 large onion, thinly sliced
225 g/8 oz lean streaky bacon, rind removed and
chopped
1 clove garlic, crushed
100 g/4 oz red cabbage, finely shredded
1 tablespoon caraway seeds
salt and freshly ground black pepper
225 g/8 oz smoked sausage, thickly sliced
100 g/4 oz button mushrooms
300 ml/½ pint dry cider
beaten egg or milk to glaze

Make the pastry according to the recipe instructions and roll out to approximately 3.5 cm/1½ inches larger than a 1.15-litre/2-pint pie dish. Line the dampened edge of the dish with a strip of pastry.

Melt the butter in a large pan, add the onion, bacon and garlic and cook until the onion is soft but not browned. Add the cabbage and caraway seeds and season lightly. Cook for a few minutes then stir in the sausage, mushrooms and cider. Pour into the pie dish, dampen the pastry rim with water and cover with the pastry lid. Seal the edges and cut a small hole in the top of the pie to allow any steam to escape. Brush with a little beaten egg or milk and bake in a hot oven (220°C, 425°F, Gas Mark 7) for 30 minutes until golden brown. Serve hot. *Serves 4–6*

Savoury Horns

½ quantity Puff pastry (see page 49)
beaten egg or milk to glaze
225 g/8 oz cream cheese
freshly ground black pepper
50 g/2 oz salami, chopped
2 spring onions, chopped
25 g/1 oz black olives, chopped
3 rashers lean bacon, rind removed and chopped
1 canned pineapple ring, chopped
1 tablespoon chopped pimiento
Garnish
10 black olives
sprigs of parsley

Grease a baking tray. Make the pastry according to the recipe instructions and roll out to a 30-cm/12-inch square. Trim the edges of the pastry and cut into 1-cm/½-inch strips. Dampen the strips of pastry down one edge with a little water. Wrap the strips around cream horn tins with a dampened edge overlapping on the underside. Place on the baking tray and brush with a little beaten egg or milk and bake in a hot oven (220°C, 425°F, Gas Mark 7) for 10–12 minutes until well puffed and golden brown. Allow to cool slightly before removing the tins.

Season the cream cheese with freshly ground black pepper and divide into two equal portions. Mix the salami, spring onions and chopped olives into one portion and use to fill half of the pastry horns.

Grill the bacon until crisp, drain on absorbent kitchen paper and mix with the remaining cream cheese, pineapple and pimiento. Use this mixture to fill the remaining pastry horns.

Garnish the savoury horns with whole black olives and small sprigs of parsley. *Makes 20*

Kidneys en Croûte

An unusual starter for a light main course or a tasty lunch or supper dish.

$\frac{1}{2}$ quantity Puff pastry (see page 49)
4 lambs' kidneys (approximately 225 g/8 oz in weight)
4 rashers lean bacon, rinds removed
salt and freshly ground black pepper
2 tablespoons chopped mixed fresh herbs (for example parsley, thyme or sage)
beaten egg or milk to glaze

Grease two baking trays. Make the pastry according to the recipe instructions and roll out thinly to a rectangle measuring approximately 20 × 50 cm/8 × 20 inches. Use a 10-cm/4-inch pastry cutter to cut out eight rounds of pastry.

Wrap each kidney in a rasher of bacon and place on a round of pastry. Season and sprinkle with chopped herbs then dampen the edges of the pastry with water and place another round of pastry on top. Seal the edges and use any pastry trimmings to decorate the tops. Place on the baking trays and brush with beaten egg or milk and bake in a hot oven (220°C, 425°F, Gas Mark 7) for 25–30 minutes.
Makes 4

Mushroom Puffs with Stilton Dressing

(Illustrated on page 54)
These little puffs make a delicious starter or are ideal for buffet parties.

½ quantity Puff pastry (see page 49)
18 medium to large button mushrooms
oil for deep frying
Dressing
100 g/4 oz Stilton cheese, finely grated
150 ml/¼ pint natural yogurt
1 tablespoon chopped fresh chives

Make the pastry according to the recipe instructions and roll out to a 30-cm/12-inch square. Cut the square into six 10 × 15-cm/4 × 6-inch strips. Cut across these strips to give 36 (5-cm/2-inch) squares.

Clean the mushrooms and place each mushroom on a square of pastry. Dampen the edges of the pastry with water and place a second pastry square on top. Seal the edges. Continue sandwiching the mushrooms in the pastry until all are used. Deep fry the squares for a few minutes until well puffed and golden brown.

To make the dressing, mash the Stilton with the yogurt until creamy. Add the chives and chill. Alternatively, liquidise the Stilton with the yogurt until smooth.

The mushroom puffs can be served hot or warm with the dressing.
Makes 18

Steak and Oyster Pie

Mouth-watering is the only way to describe this rich pie.
A traditional British dish which is not quite as
extravagant as it may sound since it uses canned oysters.

50 g/2 oz butter
225 g/8 oz small pickling onions
450 g/1 lb lean braising steak
2 tablespoons plain flour
salt and freshly ground black pepper
300 ml/½ pint beef stock
300 ml/½ pint dry red wine
100 g/4 oz button mushrooms
2 (105-g/3⅔-oz) cans smoked oysters, drained
½ quantity Puff pastry (see page 49)
beaten egg or milk to glaze

Melt the butter, add the onions and cook for a few minutes. Cut the meat into 2.5-cm/1-inch cubes and coat in the flour. Add to the onions, season generously then cook until lightly browned. Gradually stir in the stock and wine, bring to the boil and add the mushrooms. Reduce the heat, cover and simmer very gently for 1–1½ hours or until the steak is tender. Leave until cool then stir in the smoked oysters. Transfer to a 1.15-litre/2-pint pie dish.

Roll out the puff pastry to give a piece approximately 3.5 cm/1½ inches larger than the top of the dish. Cut a 2.5-cm/1-inch strip from the edge of the pastry and use to line the dampened rim of the pie dish. Dampen the pastry rim with water and cover with the rolled-out pastry lid. Trim and seal the edges and use any pastry trimmings to decorate the pie. Brush with a little beaten egg or milk and bake in a hot oven (230°C, 450°F, Gas Mark 8) for 20–30 minutes until well puffed and golden brown. Serve immediately. *Serves 6*

Banana Bacon Savouries

(Illustrated on page 17)
*These rolls are ideal for parties or buffet meals or why
not serve them as an unusual starter?*

½ quantity Puff, Flaky or Rough puff pastry
(see pages 48–50)
5 bananas
juice of 1 lemon
350 g/12 oz lean bacon, rind removed
beaten egg or milk to glaze

Make the pastry according to the recipe instructions. Roll out to
a rectangle measuring 45 × 60 cm/18 × 24 inches. Trim the edges
and cut into strips measuring approximately 3.5 × 45 cm/1½ × 18
inches. Cut the strips in half so that they measure 23 cm/9 inches in
length.
 Cut each banana into six pieces and dip in the lemon juice. Wrap
each piece of banana in half a rasher of bacon and wrap in a strip of
pastry, dampening the end with water to seal. Place on dampened
baking trays and brush with a little beaten egg or milk. Bake in a hot
oven (230°C, 450°F, Gas Mark 8) for 10–15 minutes. Serve warm or
cold. *Makes 30*

Smoked Salmon and Cucumber Vol-au-vent

This is ideal to serve on hot summer days. Serve with minted new potatoes and a tomato salad. An excellent dish to serve at a wedding breakfast.

$\frac{1}{2}$ quantity Puff pastry (see page 49)
beaten egg or milk to glaze
225 g/8 oz smoked salmon pieces
$\frac{1}{2}$ cucumber, peeled and diced
salt and freshly ground black pepper
2 spring onions, finely chopped
grated rind of I lemon
150 ml/$\frac{1}{4}$ pint soured cream
I tablespoon chopped parsley

Make the pastry according to the recipe instructions. Divide in half and roll each piece out to an 18-cm/7-inch round. Place one circle of pastry on a dampened baking tray. Cut out a circle measuring 13 cm/5 inches from the middle of the second round. Dampen the outer edge of the ring of pastry with water and neatly press around the edge of the circle of pastry on the baking tray. Prick the middle of the vol-au-vent all over with a fork. Glaze the rim, taking care not to get any beaten egg or milk around the edges of the pastry as this prevents it from rising. Place the smaller circle of pastry (the lid) on another dampened baking tray and brush with beaten egg or milk. Bake in a hot oven (230°C, 450°F, Gas Mark 8) for 15–20 minutes. Cool on a wire rack.

Roughly chop the smoked salmon. Sprinkle the cucumber with a little salt and leave for 10 minutes. Drain and dry thoroughly then mix with the salmon, spring onion, lemon rind and seasoning. Stir in the soured cream and parsley and use to fill the cooled vol-au-vent. Place the lid on top at a slight angle. *Serves 4*

Savoury Pinwheels

(Illustrated on page 17)
$\frac{1}{2}$ quantity Puff pastry (see page 49)
2 (120-g/4$\frac{1}{4}$-oz) cans sardines in oil
100 g/4 oz full-fat soft cheese
1 teaspoon dried chives
rind and juice of 1 lemon

Grease a baking tray. Make the pastry according to the recipe instructions and roll out to an oblong measuring 35 × 18 cm/ 14 × 7 inches. Mash the sardines with their oil then beat in the remaining ingredients and spread evenly over the pastry. Roll up from the long side to give a 35-cm/14-inch long roll. Chill thoroughly. Cut the roll vertically into 36 slices, place well apart on the baking tray and bake in a moderately hot oven (200°C, 400°F, Gas Mark 6) for 10–15 minutes. *Makes 36*

Variation
Bacon and Onion Pinwheels: Finely chop 1 small onion and 50 g/2 oz lean bacon. Melt 25 g/1 oz butter in a pan and sauté the bacon and onion until just cooked. Cool. Beat into 100 g/4 oz full-fat soft cheese and use as above.

Chicken Liver Turnovers

½ quantity Puff pastry (see page 49)
25 g/1 oz butter
1 small onion, finely chopped
225 g/8 oz lean bacon, rind removed and finely chopped
225 g/8 oz chicken livers, trimmed and finely chopped
1 teaspoon powdered sage
salt and freshly ground black pepper
beaten egg or milk to glaze

Make the pastry according to the recipe instructions and roll out to a 40-cm/16-inch square. Cut into four 20-cm/8-inch squares. Melt the butter in a frying pan, add the onion and cook until the onion is soft but not browned. Add the bacon and liver and continue to cook, stirring continuously, until the liver has changed colour. Add the sage to the filling and season well. Cool.

Place a quarter of the filling on each of the pastry squares and dampen the edges with water. Fold one side of the pastry over the filling to form a triangle. Brush with beaten egg or milk and place on a dampened baking tray. Bake in a moderately hot oven (200°C, 400°F, Gas Mark 6) until well puffed and golden brown. *Makes 4*

Beef and Walnut Pie

(Illustrated on page 71)
This full-flavoured succulent pie is worthy of any special guest.

675 g/1½ lb braising steak
50 g/2 oz butter
1 large onion, sliced
100 g/4 oz walnut halves
salt and freshly ground black pepper
25 g/1 oz plain flour
pared rind of 1 large orange
2 bay leaves
600 ml/1 pint beef stock
½ quantity Puff pastry (see page 49)
beaten egg or milk to glaze

Trim any fat from the steak and cut into 2.5-cm/1-inch cubes. Melt the butter in a heavy-based saucepan or flameproof casserole, add the onion and walnuts and cook until the onion is soft but not browned. Add the meat and season generously. Cook until lightly browned then stir in the flour, orange rind and bay leaves. Gradually add the stock and bring to the boil. Reduce the heat and cook gently for 1–1½ hours or until the meat is tender. Remove the orange rind and bay leaves and cool slightly.

Make the pastry according to the recipe instructions and roll out to approximately 3.5 cm/1½ inches larger than a 1.15-litre/2-pint pie dish. Trim a 2.5-cm/1-inch strip from the edge of the pastry and use to line the dampened rim of the dish. Dampen the pastry rim with water, place the filling in the dish and cover with the pastry lid. Trim, seal and flute the edges. Use any pastry trimmings to decorate the pie. Brush with a little beaten egg or milk and bake in a hot oven (230°C, 450°F, Gas Mark 8) for 20 minutes until well puffed and golden brown. Serve immediately. *Serves 4–6*

Tuna Envelopes with Lemon Parsley Sauce

½ quantity Puff pastry (see page 49)
25 g/1 oz butter
1 medium onion, finely chopped
100 g/4 oz mushrooms, sliced
1 (198-g/7-oz) can sweetcorn kernels, drained
1 (198-g/7-oz) can tuna, drained and flaked
beaten egg or milk to glaze
Sauce
2 tablespoons cornflour
300 ml/½ pint milk
grated rind of 1 lemon
2 egg yolks
2 tablespoons chopped parsley
salt and freshly ground black pepper

Make the pastry according to the recipe instructions and roll out to a 35-cm/14-inch square. Cut the square into four 18-cm/7-inch squares.

To prepare the filling, melt the butter in a frying pan, add the onion and mushrooms and sauté gently until soft but not browned. Mix the sweetcorn, tuna and onion mixture together and divide the mixture between the squares. Dampen the edges of each square with water and join the four corners above the middle of the filling to form an envelope. Seal and pinch the edges together then brush with beaten egg or milk. Place on a dampened baking tray and cook in a moderately hot oven (200°C, 400°F, Gas Mark 6) for 20–30 minutes.

To prepare the sauce, mix the cornflour with the milk, lemon rind and egg yolks. Heat, stirring continuously, until the sauce thickens and boils. Add the parsley and season to taste. Serve with the tuna envelopes. *Makes 4*

Savoury Wrapped Pears

(Illustrated on page 54)
$\frac{1}{2}$ quantity Puff pastry (see page 49)
175 g/6 oz blue cheese, finely crumbled
50 g/2 oz full-fat soft cheese
I tablespoon finely chopped onion
4 pears
juice of I lemon
beaten egg or milk to glaze

Make the pastry according to the recipe instructions and roll out to a 30-cm/12-inch square. From this cut four 8.5-cm/3$\frac{1}{2}$-inch rounds. Use the remainder to cut pastry strips 2.5 cm/1 inch wide.

Prepare the filling for the pears by mixing the blue cheese, full-fat soft cheese and onion together. Peel the pears and remove the core from underneath. Brush with lemon juice. Stuff the cored pears with the filling and place on the rounds of pastry. Dampen the pastry strips with water then wind around the pears overlapping the pastry rounds. The strips should be well sealed together and should completely cover the pears. Use any remaining pastry to make leaves to decorate the tops of the pears. Brush with beaten egg or milk and bake in a moderately hot oven (200°C, 400°F, Gas Mark 6) for 25–30 minutes. Serve garnished with salad ingredients. *Serves 4*

Salmon Pies with Soured Cream Dressing

½ quantity Puff pastry (see page 49)
2 (213-g/7½-oz) cans salmon
25 g/1 oz butter
1 large onion, finely chopped
100 g/4 oz button mushrooms, sliced
salt and freshly ground black pepper
beaten egg or milk to glaze
150 ml/¼ pint soured cream
2 tablespoons chopped chives

Make the pastry according to the recipe instructions and divide into four equal portions. Cut each portion in half and roll one half out to a 14-cm/5½-inch circle. Use to line a 10-cm/4-inch Yorkshire pudding tin. Repeat with the remaining pastry, rolling out the remaining halves to make lids.

Flake the salmon into a bowl removing the skin and bones. Melt the butter in a frying pan and sauté the onion until soft but not browned. Add the onion and mushrooms to the salmon and season to taste. Divide the filling into four and place in the pastry-lined Yorkshire pudding tins. Dampen the edges of the pastry with water and cover each pie with a lid, sealing the edges well. Use any pastry trimmings to decorate the pies. Brush with a little beaten egg or milk and bake in a hot oven (220°C, 425°F, Gas Mark 7) for 15 minutes, then reduce the oven temperature to moderately hot (190°C, 375°F, Gas Mark 5) and continue to cook for a further 15–20 minutes. Meanwhile make the dressing by mixing the soured cream with the chives. Serve the pies hot or cold with the dressing. *Makes 4*

Variation

Mackerel Pies with Horseradish Dressing: Replace the salmon with 450 g/1 lb cooked, boned mackerel. Serve with a sauce made from 2 tablespoons creamed horseradish and 150 ml/¼ pint soured cream.

York Fingers

$\frac{1}{2}$ quantity Puff pastry (see page 49)
275 g/10 oz mature Cheddar cheese, thinly sliced
225 g/8 oz sliced ham
beaten egg or milk to glaze
50 g/2 oz Cheddar cheese, finely grated

Make the pastry according to the recipe instructions and roll out to a 40-cm/16-inch square. Cut the square into four 40 × 10-cm/ 16 × 4-inch rectangles. On two of the rectangles of pastry place a layer of sliced cheese and ham and place the other two rectangles on top. Brush with beaten egg or milk and sprinkle with the grated cheese. Cut the rectangles into 32 (2.5 × 10-cm/1 × 4-inch) fingers. Place on a dampened baking tray and bake in a hot oven (230°C, 450°F, Gas Mark 8) for 5 minutes until puffed and golden brown. *Makes 32*

Opposite Beef and Walnut Pie (see page 66); Pork Pie with Peaches (see page 95); Spiced Lamb Pudding (see page 83).
Overleaf Lemon Fish Pie (see page 22); Prawn Mille Feuilles (see page 52); Fisherman's Pudding (see page 85); Lemon Turkey Pie (see page 96); Almond Apple Squares (see page 77); Picnic Pie (see page 99).

Gammon en Croûte

1 (1.5–1.75-kg/3½–4-lb) middle gammon joint
50 g/2 oz butter
1 large onion, finely chopped
1 large clove garlic, crushed
salt and freshly ground black pepper
grated rind of 2 oranges
1 (411-g/4½-oz) can apricot halves, drained and chopped
50 g/2 oz fresh breadcrumbs
½ quantity Puff pastry (see page 49)
beaten egg or milk to glaze

Soak the gammon for several hours in cold water. Change the water and bring the gammon to the boil in a large saucepan. Change the water again, bring to the boil and simmer gently for 1¾–2 hours. Drain, remove the skin and any excess fat and cool.

Melt the butter in a saucepan, add the onion and garlic and season generously. Cook until soft but not browned. Add the orange rind, apricot and breadcrumbs and mix thoroughly.

Make the pastry according to the recipe instructions and roll out two-thirds into a round large enough to cover the base and sides of the gammon joint (approximately 30 cm/12 inches in diameter). Place the cooled joint on the rolled-out pastry and cover all over with the stuffing. Roll out the reserved pastry to give a round large enough to cover the top of the joint (approximately 23 cm/9 inches in diameter). Dampen the edges of the pastry with water and carefully ease it up around the sides of the gammon, gently pressing it into place but leaving the top edge unsealed so that it can be later sealed to the separate pastry lid. Place the smaller round on top to serve as the lid and press the two edges together. Make a small hole in the top to allow any steam to escape and use any pastry trimmings to decorate. Place on a dampened baking tray and brush with beaten egg or milk. Bake in a hot oven (220°C, 425°F, Gas Mark 7) for 30–40 minutes until golden brown. Serve immediately. *Serves 4–6*

Lattice-topped Pork (see page 116); Bacon Casserole with Herby Choux Topping (see page 109); Braised Vegetables with Pork Dumplings (see page 86).

Vanilla Cream Slices

½ quantity Puff, Rough puff or Flaky pastry
(see pages 48–50)
25 g/1 oz cornflour
3 egg yolks
50 g/2 oz castor sugar
¾ teaspoon vanilla essence
300 ml/½ pint milk
300 ml/½ pint double cream
225 g/8 oz icing sugar, sifted

Make the pastry according to the recipe instructions, divide in half and roll out each half to a 10 × 38-cm/4 × 15-inch rectangle. Place on a dampened baking tray and cook in a hot oven (220°C, 425°F, Gas Mark 7) for 15–20 minutes. Cool and carefully split each rectangle in half horizontally.

Meanwhile prepare the filling. Mix the cornflour, egg yolks, sugar and vanilla essence together with 2 tablespoons of the milk. Heat the remainder of the milk, add to the cornflour and egg mixture. Return to the heat, stirring continuously, until the custard thickens. Do not allow to boil. Cool. Beat in 2 tablespoons of the cream. Whip the remainder of the cream and fold into the custard.

Spread each bottom half of pastry with half of the custard. Cover with the top layer of pastry and chill. Cut each rectangle into seven slices. Mix the icing sugar with enough water to make a thick glacé icing. Spread on top of the pastry and serve. *Makes 14*

Variation
The slices may also be sandwiched together with strawberry or raspberry jam as well as the custard.

Almond Apple Squares

(Illustrated on page 73)
1 quantity Puff pastry (see page 49)
2 (225-g/8-oz) packets marzipan
2 large cooking apples, peeled and cored
milk to glaze
a few flaked almonds to decorate
icing sugar, sifted

Make the pastry according to the recipe instructions and roll out to a 40-cm/16-inch square. Cut into 16 (10-cm/4-inch) squares. Divide the marzipan into eight equal pieces and roll each piece into a 7.5-cm/3-inch square. Place a piece of marzipan on each pastry square.

Slice each apple into four rings and place a ring on top of the marzipan. Cover with a second square of pastry, dampening with water and sealing the edges well. Brush with milk and sprinkle with flaked almonds. Bake in a hot oven (220°C, 425°F, Gas Mark 7) for 20 minutes. Sprinkle with sifted icing sugar. Serve warm or cold with lightly-whipped double cream. *Makes 8*

Mincemeat and Apricot Jalousie

(Illustrated on pages 102–3)
½ quantity Puff pastry (see page 49)
225 g/8 oz mincemeat
225 g/8 oz dried apricots, soaked overnight in water
grated rind of I lemon
50 g/2 oz flaked almonds
milk to glaze

Make the pastry according to the recipe instructions and divide in half. Roll out each piece of pastry to a rectangle measuring 12 × 30 cm/5 × 12 inches. Spread the mincemeat over the centre of one piece of pastry and arrange the drained apricots on top. Sprinkle the lemon rind and half of the flaked almonds over the mincemeat. Gently fold the remaining piece of pastry in half lengthways and cut diagonal slits through the folded edge but leaving the open edge un-cut. Carefully open out the pastry. Dampen the edges of the pastry base with water and place the cut pastry piece on top. Seal the edges well. Brush with a little milk and sprinkle the remaining flaked almonds over the top. Bake in a hot oven (220°C, 425°F, Gas Mark 7) for 25–30 minutes until golden and well puffed. *Serves 4–6*

Apricot Horns

(Illustrated on page 35)
$\frac{1}{2}$ quantity Puff pastry (see page 49)
milk to glaze
icing sugar, sifted
Cream Filling
1 (411-g/14$\frac{1}{2}$-oz) can apricots
25 g/1 oz icing sugar, sifted
300 ml/$\frac{1}{2}$ pint double cream
grated rind of 1 orange

Make the pastry according to the recipe instructions and roll out to a 45 × 13-cm/18 × 5-inch rectangle. Trim the edges and cut the rectangle into ten 1-cm/$\frac{1}{2}$-inch wide strips along the length. Dampen the cream horn tins and one edge of each strip of pastry with water. Wind one of the strips around a cream horn tin, starting at the pointed end, overlapping the dampened edge of the pastry until it is completely used. Brush with milk. Repeat with the remaining strips of pastry and cream horn tins and place on a dampened baking tray. Cook in a hot oven (220°C, 425°F, Gas Mark 7) for 15–20 minutes. Carefully remove the tins immediately the horns come out of the oven. Cool on a wire rack.

Meanwhile prepare the filling. Drain and chop the apricots. Add the icing sugar to the cream together with the grated orange rind. Whip until stiff and stir in the chopped apricots. Fill the cream horns with this mixture. Dust with icing sugar. Serve within 2–3 hours of filling. *Makes 10*

CHAPTER 4

Suet Crust Pastry

*Suet crust pastry should be light and spongy when cooked.
It should be kneaded quickly on a well-floured surface
before being used and is normally covered and then
steamed or baked. This recipe produces enough pastry to
line and cover a 1.15-litre/2-pint pudding basin and is
referred to as 'I quantity' throughout this chapter.*

225 g/8 oz self-raising flour
generous pinch of salt
100 g/4 oz shredded suet
175 ml/6 fl oz cold water

Place the flour in a bowl with the salt. Add the suet, stirring it in
lightly. Lightly mix in the water to form a soft dough. Knead lightly
on a floured surface and use as required.

Ham and Mushroom Roly-Poly

I quantity Suet crust pastry (see opposite)
25 g/I oz butter
2 cloves garlic, crushed
I large onion, chopped
100 g/4 oz button mushrooms, coarsely chopped
225 g/8 oz cooked ham, coarsely chopped
salt and freshly ground black pepper
beaten egg or milk to glaze
2 tablespoons sesame seeds

Grease a baking tray. Make the pastry according to the recipe instructions and roll out to an oblong measuring 25×20 cm/ 10×8 inches.

Melt the butter, add the garlic and onion and cook until soft but not browned. Stir in the mushrooms and ham and season generously, then cool.

Spread the filling over the pastry and fold the outer I cm/$\frac{1}{2}$ inch of the edge over it. Carefully roll up from the long end sealing the edges and place on the baking tray. Brush with a little beaten egg or milk and press the sesame seeds all over the roll. Bake in a moderately hot oven (190°C, 375°F, Gas Mark 5) for 45–50 minutes until golden brown and cooked through. Serve immediately. *Serves 6*

Chicken Pudding

A delicious pudding worthy of serving to any guest on a cold winter's evening.

675 g/1½ lb uncooked chicken meat
50 g/2 oz butter
225 g/8 oz small pickling onions
salt and freshly ground black pepper
2 tablespoons plain flour
300 ml/½ pint dry white wine
½ chicken stock cube
100 g/4 oz button mushrooms
I quantity Suet crust pastry (see page 80)

Grease a 1.15-litre/2-pint pudding basin. Cut the chicken into large chunks. Melt the butter in a saucepan, add the chicken and onions. Season and sauté, stirring continuously, until the chicken meat is firm but not browned. Stir in the flour and gradually add the wine together with the stock cube, stirring to ensure that the cube dissolves. Bring to the boil, stir in the mushrooms and allow to cool.

Meanwhile, make the pastry according to the recipe instructions and roll out to a circle which is approximately 7.5 cm/3 inches larger than the diameter of the pudding basin. Cut one quarter out of the circle and use the large piece of pastry to line the pudding basin, carefully dampening the edges of pastry with water and sealing where they meet. Form the reserved pastry into a round and roll out to a circle large enough to cover the pudding.

Place the cooled filling in the pudding basin. Dampen the edges of the pastry with water and place the pastry cover on top. Press the edges together to seal. Cover with greased greaseproof paper and a piece of aluminium cooking foil. Steam for 1½–2 hours. Turn out and serve immediately. *Serves 4*

Spiced Lamb Pudding

(Illustrated on page 71)
675 g/1½ lb lean lamb
50 g/2 oz butter
1 large onion, chopped
2 tablespoons grated root ginger
2 large cloves garlic, crushed
2 cloves
2 tablespoons plain flour
salt and freshly ground black pepper
2 bay leaves
thinly-pared rind of 1 lemon
300 ml/½ pint chicken stock
2 carrots, sliced
1 quantity Suet crust pastry (see page 80)
Garnish
lemon wedges
sprigs of watercress

Cut the lamb into 2.5-cm/1-inch cubes. Melt the butter in a sauce-pan. Add the onion, root ginger, garlic and cloves. Cook for a few minutes then add the meat and cook until lightly browned. Stir in the flour and season generously. Add the bay leaves and lemon rind then stir in the stock. Bring to the boil. Add the sliced carrots. Leave until cool.

Make the pastry according to the recipe instructions and use to line a 1.15-litre/2-pint pudding basin (see page 84, Steak and Kidney Pudding). Place the lamb mixture in the basin and cover with the pastry lid, fold down and seal the edges then cover with a double piece of greased aluminium cooking foil. Fold the foil neatly around the edges of the basin to seal. Steam for 2 hours, turn out and serve immediately garnished with lemon wedges and sprigs of watercress. *Serves 4–6*

Steak and Kidney Pudding

2 tablespoons oil
225 g/8 oz button onions
450 g/1 lb stewing steak, cut into 2.5-cm/1-inch cubes
100 g/4 oz ox kidney, cut into small pieces
2 tablespoons plain flour
300 ml/$\frac{1}{2}$ pint dry red wine
1 beef stock cube, dissolved in 2 tablespoons hot water
175 g/6 oz button mushrooms
salt and freshly ground black pepper
1 quantity Suet crust pastry (see page 80)

Heat the oil in a frying pan and sauté the onions, steak and kidney until lightly browned. Add the flour and continue to cook for a further 2 minutes. Gradually blend in the red wine and stock. Bring to the boil, stirring continuously, until the sauce thickens. Cover and simmer for 30 minutes. Add the mushrooms, season to taste and cool.

Make the pastry according to the recipe instructions and reserve one quarter for the lid. Roll out the remainder to a round approximately 7.5 cm/3 inches larger than the top of a 1.15-litre/2-pint pudding basin. Grease the basin well and lightly dust the pastry with flour. Fold loosely in half and then in quarters. Lift into the basin, unfold and press neatly around the sides and edges of the dish.

Place the filling in the basin, dampen the pastry edge with water and top with the pastry lid, sealing the edges well. Cover the basin with a double piece of greased aluminium cooking foil and steam for 2$\frac{1}{2}$–3 hours. *Serves 4–6*

Fisherman's Pudding

(Illustrated on page 72)
This flavoursome fish pudding is delicious served with
buttered peas and creamy potatoes.

I quantity Suet crust pastry (see page 80)
grated rind of 2 lemons
25 g/I oz butter
I large onion, chopped
100 g/4 oz button mushrooms, sliced
2 bay leaves
juice of I small lemon
salt and freshly ground black pepper
450 g/I lb smoked haddock fillets, skinned and flaked
I tablespoon chopped parsley
150 ml/¼ pint water

Make the pastry according to the recipe instructions adding the lemon rind to the flour and suet before mixing in the water. Use to line a 1.15-litre/2-pint pudding basin (see opposite, Steak and Kidney Pudding).

Melt the butter in a pan, add the onion and cook until soft but not browned. Add the mushrooms, bay leaves and lemon juice and season sparingly. Stir in the fish, making sure that all bones are removed, then add the parsley and water.

Turn the fish mixture into the prepared basin and cover with the pastry lid. Dampen and seal the edges then cover with a double piece of greased aluminium cooking foil. Wrap the edges of the foil firmly around the rim of the basin to seal and steam for 1½–2 hours. Turn out and serve immediately. *Serves 4–6*

Braised Vegetables with Pork Dumplings

(Illustrated on page 74)
This moist casserole is a complete meal in itself. Serve in
heated bowls accompanied by crisp, hot French bread.

2 tablespoons sesame or cooking oil
I small onion, finely chopped
225 g/8 oz minced pork
50 g/2 oz streaky bacon, rind removed and chopped
I teaspoon chopped fresh rosemary
grated rind of I orange
4 tablespoons fresh breadcrumbs
salt and freshly ground black pepper
I quantity Suet crust pastry (see page 80)
50 g/2 oz butter
6 sticks celery, sliced
225 g/8 oz carrots, sliced
450 g/I lb leeks, sliced
1.15 litres/2 pints chicken stock

Heat the oil in a pan, add the onion and cook until soft but not
browned. Add the pork and bacon and cook until lightly browned.
Remove from the heat and stir in the rosemary, orange rind and
breadcrumbs. Season generously.

Make the pastry according to the recipe instructions and divide
into eight pieces. Roll out each piece to a 7.5-cm/3-inch round.
Divide the meat mixture into eight portions and place one portion
in the middle of each circle of pastry. Fold the pastry up over the
meat and roll into a dumpling, smoothing the pastry evenly over the
filling.

Melt the butter in a saucepan and sauté the celery, carrot and
leek gently for 2 minutes. Add the stock and bring to the boil.
Reduce the heat and arrange the dumplings on top. Cover and cook
gently for 45 minutes turning the dumplings once during cooking.
Serve immediately. *Serves 4*

Pizza Flan

25 g/1 oz butter
1 large onion, finely chopped
2 teaspoons caraway seeds
175 g/6 oz streaky bacon, rind removed and chopped
salt and freshly ground black pepper
1 quantity Suet crust pastry (see page 80)
225 g/8 oz full-fat soft cheese
450 g/1 lb tomatoes, peeled and sliced
100 g/4 oz Cheddar cheese, grated
2 (50-g/1¾-oz) cans anchovy fillets in olive oil, drained
and oil reserved
20 black olives

Melt the butter in a pan, add the onion and cook until soft but not browned. Stir in the caraway seeds, bacon and seasoning to taste.

Make the pastry according to the recipe instructions and use to line a 29 × 24-cm/11½ × 9½-inch oblong flan dish. Spread the onion mixture over the base and cut the soft cheese into chunks. Dot the cheese over the onion and top with the sliced tomatoes. Sprinkle with the grated cheese and arrange the anchovy fillets in a lattice pattern on top. Sprinkle the oil reserved from the anchovies over the flan. Decorate with black olives and bake in a moderately hot oven (200°C, 400°F, Gas Mark 6) for 40 minutes. *Serves 6–8*

Baked Frankfurter Pudding

This unusual pudding is full-flavoured and delicious. The baked suet crust pastry becomes crisp and light and is far less trouble to cook than by the traditional steaming method.

2 large leeks, sliced
50 g/2 oz butter
1 large eating apple, peeled, cored and sliced
salt and freshly ground black pepper
1 tablespoon plain flour
150 ml/¼ pint dry cider
12 frankfurters, sliced
1 quantity Suet crust pastry (see page 80)

Wash the leek thoroughly. Melt the butter in a saucepan, add the leek and cook, stirring continuously, for 5 minutes. Add the apple and season generously then stir in the flour and cider. Add the frankfurters and cook for a few minutes. Leave to cool.

Make the pastry according to the recipe instructions and use to line a 1.15-litre/2-pint ovenproof pudding basin (see page 84, Steak and Kidney pudding). Place the filling in the basin, dampen the pastry edges with water and cover with the pastry lid. Seal the edges then make a small hole in the top of the pudding to allow any steam to escape. Bake, uncovered, in a moderately hot oven (200°C, 400°F, Gas Mark 6) for 50 minutes. Serve immediately. *Serves 4–6*

Fruit Roly-poly with Orange Sauce

1 quantity Suet crust pastry (see page 80)
100 g/4 oz dried apricots, soaked overnight in water
and chopped
50 g/2 oz raisins
50 g/2 oz glacé cherries, chopped
50 g/2 oz dates, chopped
50 g/2 oz walnuts, coarsely chopped
grated rind of 1 orange
grated rind of 1 lemon
4 tablespoons clear honey
Sauce
25 g/1 oz cornflour
300 ml/½ pint juice reserved from the apricots
50 g/2 oz castor sugar
grated rind and juice of 1 orange
2 tablespoons brandy (optional)

Grease a baking tray. Make the pastry according to the recipe instructions and roll out to a 30 × 25-cm/12 × 10-inch rectangle.

Mix the remaining eight ingredients together and spread over the pastry leaving a clear border at the edges. Turn over 1 cm/½ inch of the pastry all around the edges and roll up carefully from the long end. Place on the baking tray and cover with greased aluminium cooking foil. Bake in a moderate oven (180°C, 350°F, Gas Mark 4) for 30 minutes. Remove the foil and continue cooking for a further 15–20 minutes.

Meanwhile prepare the sauce. Blend the cornflour with a little of the reserved apricot juice, add the remainder of the juice, the sugar, orange rind and juice. Heat, stirring continuously, until the sauce boils and thickens. Stir in the brandy if used and serve with the hot roly-poly. *Serves 6–8*

Stuffed Apple Dumplings

(Illustrated on page 53)
1 quantity Suet crust pastry (see page 80)
50 g/2 oz hazelnuts, finely chopped
50 g/2 oz dates, finely chopped
50 g/2 oz soft brown sugar
grated rind of 1 orange
juice of $\frac{1}{2}$ orange
4 cooking apples, peeled and cored

Grease a baking tray. Make the pastry according to the recipe instructions and divide into four equal portions. Roll each portion out to a circle measuring 18 cm/7 inches in diameter. Reserve any pastry trimmings.

To prepare the stuffing, mix together the hazelnuts, dates, sugar, orange rind and juice. Place an apple on each piece of pastry and place a quarter of the stuffing into the centre cavity of each. Wrap up in the pastry, sealing the edges well and decorate with the pastry trimmings. Place on the baking tray and bake in a moderate oven (180°C, 350°F, Gas Mark 4) for 30–40 minutes. *Makes 4*

Lamb Curry with Banana Puffs (see page 114); Scottish Lamb Pies (see page 97); Samosas with Yogurt Dressing (see page 29).

Apple and Apricot Pudding

1 quantity Suet crust pastry (see page 80)
225 g/8 oz dried apricots, soaked overnight in water
100 g/4 oz raisins
450 g/1 lb cooking apples, peeled, cored and sliced
grated rind of 1 orange
50 g/2 oz sugar
Sauce
225 g/8 oz apricot jam
150 ml/$\frac{1}{4}$ pint dry sherry

Make the pastry according to the recipe instructions. Bring the apricots to the boil in the water in which they have been soaked. Add the raisins and cook for 20 minutes or until most of the liquid has been absorbed. Leave to cool. Add the apples to the apricots together with the orange rind and sugar.

Roll out the pastry to a circle approximately 7.5 cm/3 inches larger than the top of a 1.15-litre/2-pint pudding basin. Cut a quarter out of the circle and use the remaining three-quarters to line the basin. Place the apricot mixture in the basin and roll the remaining pastry out into a circle large enough to cover the top. Dampen the edges with water, place the pastry lid on top of the pudding and seal the edges well.

Cover the top first with greased greaseproof paper and then with a double piece of aluminium cooking foil. Steam for 1$\frac{1}{2}$ hours.

Meanwhile make the sauce. Heat the apricot jam until liquid then stir in the sherry. Serve poured over the turned-out pudding.
Serves 6

Potato Puffs (see page 117); Layered Vegetable Pie (see page 25).

CHAPTER 5

Hot Water Crust Pastry

Hot water crust pastry is crisp and ideal for savoury pies. During preparation the pastry should be kept warm and should be handled quickly and carefully with warm hands. Where the pastry is moulded over an upturned tin in the following recipes, the pastry shell should be left in a cool place until set, about 30 minutes. An alternative method of lining the inside of a loose-bottomed tin may also be used. It will be necessary however, to remove the pie from the tin, leaving it on its base, and glazing the sides with beaten egg for the last 30 minutes of the cooking time.
This recipe produces enough pastry to make a deep 15-cm/6-inch pie or to line and cover a 23-cm/9-inch raised pie mould. It is referred to as 'I quantity' throughout this chapter.

350 g/12 oz plain flour
$\frac{1}{2}$ teaspoon salt
100 g/4 oz lard
4 tablespoons water
4 tablespoons milk

Place the flour and salt in a bowl. Place the lard, water and milk in a saucepan and heat gently until the lard melts. Bring to the boil then pour on to the flour and mix in quickly. Use warm hands to knead the dough until smooth. Work quickly and carefully as the dough is very hot and needs to remain hot for use.

To keep the dough hot, place in a basin over a saucepan of hot water, cover and use as soon as possible.

Pork Pie with Peaches

(Illustrated on page 71)

*This pie is useful for cold suppers or picnics since it should
be made on the day or several hours prior to eating. Serve
with an elaborate decoration of salad ingredients.*

I quantity Hot water crust pastry (see opposite)
675 g/1½ lb lean pork
25 g/1 oz butter
I large onion, chopped
2 cloves garlic, crushed
salt and freshly ground black pepper
I (411-g/14½-oz) can peach slices, drained
½ teaspoon dried sage
beaten egg or milk to glaze

Grease a baking tray, Make the pastry according to the recipe
and keep hot in a bowl over a saucepan of boiling water.

Cut the pork into cubes. Melt the butter, add the onion and
garlic and cook until soft but not browned. Season to taste. In
another bowl mix the peaches and sage together.

Grease the outside of a 15-cm/6-inch deep cake tin. Roll out
three-quarters of the pastry to a round approximately 5 cm/2 inches
larger than the base of the tin. Place over the bottom of the upturned tin and mould it down the sides using warm hands until the
tin is completely covered in pastry. Leave until set. Wrap a double
sheet of greaseproof paper round the pastry, secure with string
and carefully remove the tin. Place the pastry case on the baking
tray and layer in the pork and peach mixture. Roll out the remaining
pastry to cover the top of the pie, dampen the edges with water and
seal. Make a hole in the top to allow any steam to escape during
cooking.

Brush with beaten egg or milk and bake in a moderate oven
(180°C, 350°F, Gas Mark 4) for 2 hours. Leave until cold then remove
the greaseproof paper and serve garnished with salad ingredients.
Serves 6

Lemon Turkey Pie

(Illustrated on page 73)
25 g/1 oz butter
1 large onion, finely chopped
grated rind of 2 lemons
3 tablespoons chopped parsley
salt and freshly ground black pepper
900 g/2 lb turkey meat
1½ quantities Hot water crust pastry (see page 94)
beaten egg or milk to glaze
15 g/½ oz powdered aspic
300 ml/½ pint boiling water
Garnish
1 lemon, sliced
small sprigs of watercress

Melt the butter, add the onion and cook until soft but not browned. Stir in the lemon rind, parsley and season generously. Thinly slice the turkey.

Make the pastry according to the recipe instructions and use to line a 23-cm/9-inch raised pie mould (see page 98, Rabbit Pie). Layer the turkey and onion mixture in the pie. Dampen the pastry rim with water, cover with the pastry lid, dampen the edges with water and press together well to seal. Trim away any excess pastry. Cut a hole in the top to allow any steam to escape and use any pastry trimmings to decorate the pie. Brush with beaten egg or milk and bake in a moderately hot oven (200°C, 400°F, Gas Mark 6) for 40 minutes.

Remove the sides of the mould and brush the sides of the pie with a little beaten egg or milk. Bake in a moderate oven (180°C, 350°F, Gas Mark 4) for a further 40 minutes. Cover the top of the pie with a piece of aluminium cooking foil if it becomes too brown during cooking.

When the pie has cooled, dissolve the aspic in the boiling water, cool slightly then pour carefully into the pie through the hole in the top. Leave in a cool place until set. Serve garnished with lemon slices and small sprigs of watercress. *Serves 8–10*

Scottish Lamb Pies

(Illustrated on page 91)
These little pies are a scrumptious variation on the
traditional Scottish favourite — mutton pies. Serve them
hot with a rich gravy and vegetables or cold with salad.

2 tablespoons oil
I small onion, finely chopped
I small carrot, diced
I small potato, diced
450 g/I lb lean lamb, finely diced
4 tablespoons chicken stock
salt and freshly ground black pepper
I quantity Hot water crust pastry (see page 94)
beaten egg or milk to glaze

Grease a baking tray. Heat the oil in a frying pan and gently sauté
the onion until soft but not browned. Add the carrot, potato and
lamb and continue to cook until the meat is lightly browned. Add
the stock and season well. Leave until cool.

Make the pastry according to the recipe instructions and divide
into six equal portions. Reserve one-third of each portion and roll
the remainder to a 14-cm/5½-inch round. Cover the upturned
bases of six jam jars with aluminium cooking foil or cling film and
mould a circle of pastry round each. Tie a double band of greaseproof paper round the pastry and leave in a cool place until set.
Carefully remove the pastry cases from the jam jars leaving the
greaseproof band round the outside. Remove the foil or cling film
and place each pie on the baking tray. Divide the filling between the
pies and roll out the reserved pastry to make lids. Dampen the
pastry rims with water. Place the lids on top of the pies sealing the
edges well. Make a small hole in the top of each pie to allow any
steam to escape and brush with a little beaten egg or milk. Bake in a
moderately hot oven (200°C, 400°F, Gas Mark 6) for 20 minutes.

Remove the greaseproof band and glaze the sides of the pies with
beaten egg or milk. Continue cooking for a further 15–20 minutes.
Serve hot or cold. *Makes 6*

Rabbit Pie

To make a deliciously rich game pie a pheasant may be substituted for the rabbit. The bird should be boned and the meat cut into bite-sized pieces.

450 g/1 lb boneless rabbit
450 g/1 lb lean pork
50 g/2 oz butter
1 large onion, chopped
600 ml/1 pint dry red wine
salt and freshly ground black pepper
4 bay leaves
1½ quantities Hot water crust pastry (see page 94)
beaten egg or milk to glaze

Cut the rabbit and pork into 2.5-cm/1-inch cubes. Melt the butter in a saucepan, add the onion and meats and cook until just browned. Stir in the wine, seasoning to taste and the bay leaves. Bring to the boil, cover and simmer for 45 minutes. Leave until cool then remove the bay leaves.

Make the pastry according to the recipe instructions and keep one-third hot in a basin over a saucepan of boiling water. Using warm hands and working quickly, roll out the remaining pastry to give an oval shape slightly larger than the top of a 23-cm/9-inch raised pie mould. Dust the inside of the mould with flour and place the pastry over the top. Keeping the edge of the pastry around the inside edge of the tin, gently mould the pastry down the sides and base to cover the inside of the tin completely and evenly. Fill with the cooled meat mixture, pressing down well and adding any jellied stock with the meat.

Roll out the remaining pastry to give an oval slightly larger than the top of the tin. Cover the pie with the pastry and press the dampened edges together well to seal. Trim the edges and cut a small hole in the top of the pie to allow any steam to escape. Pinch the edges of the pie to seal and use the trimmings to make leaves for decoration. Brush with beaten egg or milk and bake in a moderately hot oven (200°C, 400°F, Gas Mark 6) for 40 minutes.

Carefully remove the sides of the mould and brush the sides of the pie with beaten egg or milk. Reduce the oven temperature to moderate (180°C, 350°F, Gas Mark 4) and bake for a further 45–60 minutes. Cover the top of the pie with a piece of aluminium cooking foil if it becomes too brown during cooking. Serve cold. *Serves 8–10*

Picnic Pie

(Illustrated on page 73)
225 g/8 oz minced pork
225 g/8 oz minced beef
1 tablespoon powdered sage
2 tablespoons grated root ginger (optional)
25 g/1 oz butter
2 cloves garlic, crushed
1 large onion, chopped
1 large green pepper, seeded and chopped
salt and freshly ground black pepper
1 quantity Hot water crust pastry (see page 94)
4 eggs, hard-boiled
beaten egg or milk to glaze

Mix the pork and beef with the sage and root ginger, if used. Melt the butter in a pan, add the garlic and onion and cook for a few minutes until the onion is just soft. Add the green pepper and stir into the meat mixture. Season generously.

Make the pastry according to the recipe instructions and use two-thirds to line a 1-kg/2-lb loaf tin. Place half of the meat in the bottom of the tin and arrange the whole eggs on top. Cover with the remaining meat and roll out the reserved pastry to form a lid. Place the lid on the pie, trim and seal the dampened edges. Use any pastry trimmings to decorate the pie. Brush with beaten egg or milk and bake in a moderate oven (180°C, 350°F, Gas Mark 4) for 2½–3 hours until well browned. Allow to cool in the tin then carefully turn out while the pie is still warm. *Serves 8–10*

Individual Sausagemeat Pies

1 quantity Hot water crust pastry (see page 94)
450 g/1 lb pork sausagemeat
1 large onion, finely chopped
½ teaspoon dried sage
½ teaspoon dried thyme
100 g/4 oz lean bacon, rind removed and finely chopped
salt and freshly ground black pepper
beaten egg or milk to glaze

Make the pastry according to the recipe instructions and divide into four equal pieces. Reserve a quarter of each piece for a lid and keep hot in a basin over boiling water. Closely cover the bottoms of four jam jars with aluminium cooking foil or cling film. Roll out each piece of pastry to an 18-cm/7-inch round. Mould over each jam jar and secure a double band of greaseproof paper round the pastry. Leave in the refrigerator until the pastry sets.

Mix the sausagemeat with the onion, herbs, bacon and seasoning. Carefully ease the foil and pastry off the jam jars and gently take the foil from the inside of the pastry. Fill with the sausagemeat mixture. Roll out the reserved pastry pieces to form lids, place on the pies, trim the edges and pinch them together to seal. Decorate with any pastry trimmings and brush with beaten egg or milk. Bake in a moderately hot oven (200°C, 400°F, Gas Mark 6) for 20 minutes. Remove from the oven and carefully cut away the greaseproof paper. Brush the sides of the pies with beaten egg or milk and bake for a further 20–30 minutes. Serve cold. *Makes 4*

Opposite Cherry Choux Ring (see page 120); Strawberry Choux Gâteau (see page 121); Coffee and Walnut Buns (see page 119).
Overleaf Quiche Lorraine (see page 32); Gingered Profiteroles (see page 124); Mincemeat and Apricot Jalousie (see page 78).

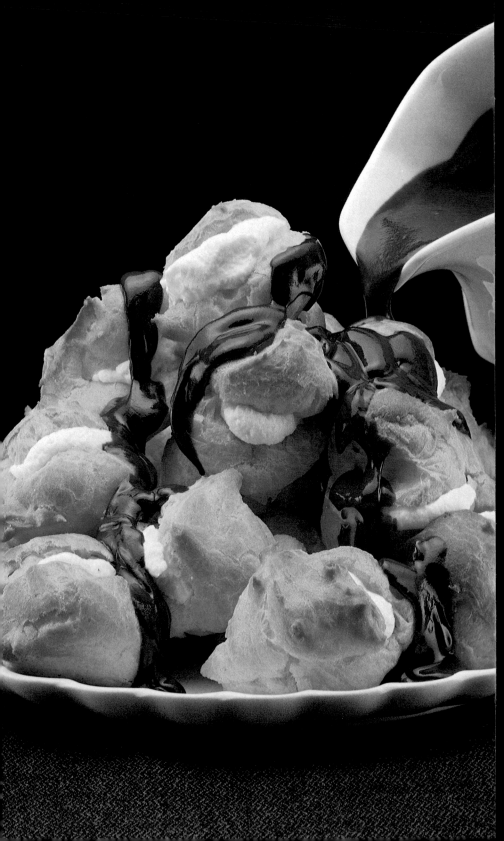

Pâté Pie

450 g/1 lb lean pork
225 g/8 oz chicken livers
50 g/2 oz butter
3 cloves garlic, crushed
1 large onion, chopped
salt and freshly ground black pepper
1 teaspoon ground nutmeg
4 tablespoons brandy
1 quantity Hot water crust pastry (see page 94)
beaten egg or milk to glaze

Cut the pork into 2.5-cm/1-inch cubes. Trim and coarsely chop the chicken livers and add to the pork. Melt the butter in a frying pan, add the garlic and onion and cook until soft but not browned. Add the pork and chicken livers and season generously. Cook until lightly browned then add the nutmeg and brandy. Heat for a few seconds then set the brandy alight. Cool then mince coarsely.

Make the pastry according to the recipe instructions. Turn a 15-cm/6-inch round deep cake tin upside down and cover closely with aluminium cooking foil or cling film. Roll out two-thirds of the pastry to a 25-cm/10-inch round. Place over the tin and carefully mould down around the sides. Tie a double band of greaseproof paper round the outside of the pastry and leave in a cool place until set. Carefully ease the pastry off the tin and remove the foil or cling film. Place the pastry case on a baking tray and press the filling firmly into the shell. Roll out the reserved pastry and use to cover the top of the pie, pressing the dampened edges together well to seal. Trim the edges and use any pastry cuttings to decorate the pie. Brush with a little beaten egg or milk.

Bake in a moderately hot oven (200°C, 400°F, Gas Mark 6) for 40 minutes then carefully remove the greaseproof paper. Brush the sides of the pie with beaten egg or milk and continue to bake in a moderate oven (180°C, 350°F, Gas Mark 4) for a further 50–60 minutes. Serve cold garnished with salad ingredients. *Serves 8–10*

Chocolate Profiteroles (see page 124).

Veal and Olive Pie

50 g/2 oz butter
2 onions, finely chopped
225 g/8 oz lean bacon, rind removed and chopped
salt and freshly ground black pepper
1.25 kg/2½ lb pie veal
300 ml/½ pint dry red wine
100 g/4 oz stuffed green olives, halved
1½ quantities Hot water crust pastry (see page 94)
beaten egg or milk to glaze
15 g/½ oz aspic powder

Melt the butter in a saucepan, add the onion and bacon and cook until the onion is soft but not browned. Season generously. Trim the veal and cut into 2.5-cm/1-inch cubes. Add to the onion and cook for a few minutes. Stir in the wine and bring to the boil then cook gently for 10 minutes. Add the olives and leave until cool.

Make the pastry according to the recipe instructions. Closely cover the outside of an upside-down 18-cm/7-inch deep cake tin with aluminium cooking foil. Knead the pastry and reserve one-third for a lid. Keep warm in a basin over a pan of boiling water. Roll out the remainder to a round just large enough to cover the base of the tin. Working quickly, using warm hands mould the pastry evenly over the tin. Tie a double band of greaseproof paper round the sides of the pastry and leave until the pastry has set. Carefully lift the tin out of the pastry shell and remove the foil.

Place the shell on a baking tray and fill with the veal mixture, adding some of the cooled cooking liquid. Reserve the remaining liquid. Roll out the reserved pastry to make a lid and place on top of the pie. Dampen and seal the edges and pinch them together to decorate.

Cut a cross in the top of the pie and fold out the four corners to leave a large hole. Mould any trimmings into leaves and arrange these radiating from the hole until only a small opening is left. Place a small ball of pastry over the opening and brush the pie with beaten egg or milk. Bake in a moderate oven (180°C, 350°F, Gas Mark 4) for 2 hours then carefully remove the paper, brush the sides of the pie with egg or milk and bake for a further 20–30 minutes. Cover the top of the pie with a piece of aluminium cooking foil if it becomes too brown during cooking. Allow to cool.

Measure 300 ml/½ pint of the reserved cooking liquid into a saucepan and bring to the boil. Dissolve the aspic in the liquid and remove the ball of pastry from the top of the pie. Carefully pour as much of the liquid as possible into the pie. Leave in a cool place until set. Serve with an elaborate decoration of salad ingredients. *Serves 6–8*

Bacon Pasties

225 g/8 oz garlic sausage
225 g/8 oz lean bacon, rind removed
I onion, finely chopped
salt and freshly ground black pepper
I quantity Hot water crust pastry (see page 94)
beaten egg or milk to glaze

Grease two baking trays. Finely chop or coarsely mince the garlic sausage and bacon. Mix with the onion and season lightly. Mix thoroughly until the ingredients bind together.

Make the pastry according to the recipe instructions and divide into eight equal portions. Divide the filling into eight portions. Roll each piece of pastry out to a 13-cm/5-inch square. Place a portion of the filling on one half of the pastry, dampen the edges and fold the other half over. Seal the edges and use any pastry trimmings to decorate the pasties. Place on the baking trays, brush with beaten egg or milk and bake in a moderately hot oven (190°C, 375°F, Gas Mark 5) for 30–40 minutes. Cool on a wire rack and serve cold with a mixed salad and small baked or new potatoes. *Makes 8*

CHAPTER 6

Choux Pastry

Choux pastry should be well puffed, crisp and golden on the outside with a moist hollow centre. To ensure success it is important that the water and fat are heated gently until the fat melts before boiling. This recipe makes enough paste for 12 éclairs, 40 small cocktail buns, 20 profiteroles or 10–12 large puffs and is referred to as '1 quantity' throughout this chapter.

150 ml/¼ pint water
50 g/2 oz butter or margarine
75 g/3 oz plain flour
pinch of salt
2 eggs, lightly beaten

Place the water in a saucepan with the butter or margarine and heat gently until the butter melts then bring rapidly to the boil. Mix the flour with the salt and add to the water immediately it boils. Beat quickly to form a smooth paste which comes away from the sides of the pan to form a ball. Cool until warm. Gradually beat the eggs into the paste then beat vigorously to give a smooth glossy mixture. Use as required.

Bacon Casserole with Herby Choux Topping

(Illustrated on page 74)
50 g/2 oz butter
1 large onion, finely chopped
1 clove garlic, crushed
2 tablespoons tomato purée
1 (450-g/1-lb) pre-packed lean bacon joint
1 leek, sliced
1 carrot, chopped
1 (227-g/8-oz) can tomatoes
300 ml/$\frac{1}{2}$ pint Guinness
salt and freshly ground black pepper
Topping
1 quantity Choux pastry (see opposite)
50 g/2 oz Cheddar cheese, finely grated
$\frac{1}{2}$ teaspoon mixed herbs

Melt the butter in a frying pan, add the onion and garlic and cook until they are soft but not browned. Add the tomato purée and continue to cook for a further 5 minutes. Cut the bacon into 2.5-cm/1-inch cubes and add to the pan together with the leek and carrot. Continue to sauté, stirring frequently, for a further 5 minutes. Add the tomatoes with their juice and the Guinness. Season well and simmer for 20 minutes over a low heat. Transfer to a 1.8-litre/3-pint ovenproof casserole.

Meanwhile prepare the topping. Make the pastry according to the recipe instructions, adding the cheese and herbs with the lightly-beaten eggs. Place the pastry in a piping bag fitted with a plain nozzle and pipe choux buns round the edge of the casserole on top of the meat. Cook in a hot oven (220°C, 425°F, Gas Mark 7) for 20 minutes, then reduce the oven temperature to moderate (180°C, 350°F, Gas Mark 4) and continue cooking for a further 20 minutes. *Serves 4*

Savoury Choux Puffs

An unusual recipe which is ideal for parties. These little buns would also make an interesting starter. The buns and their filling may be frozen separately.

I quantity Choux pastry (see page 108)
2 tablespoons chopped mixed fresh herbs (for example parsley, thyme, sage and rosemary)
225 g/8 oz chicken livers
I onion
225 g/8 oz uncooked chicken
25 g/I oz butter
2 cloves garlic, crushed
4 tablespoons brandy
300 ml/$\frac{1}{2}$ pint dry white wine
salt and freshly ground black pepper
150 ml/$\frac{1}{4}$ pint double cream
parsley sprigs to garnish

Grease two baking trays. Make the pastry according to the recipe instructions stirring in the herbs with the flour. Pipe or spoon 40 small cocktail-sized buns on to the baking trays. Bake in a hot oven (220°C, 425°F, Gas Mark 7) for 15–20 minutes. Cool on a wire rack. Make a slit in each bun immediately they are removed from the oven to allow any steam to escape.

Trim and chop the chicken livers into small pieces. Chop the onion and chicken coarsely. Melt the butter in a pan, add the garlic and prepared ingredients and cook, stirring continuously, for 10 minutes. Pour over the brandy and set alight. Leave to burn then when the flames die down add the wine and season generously. Bring to the boil and cook, covered, for 30 minutes. Liquidise until smooth and leave until cold. Lightly whip the cream and stir into the pâté. Use to fill the choux buns. Garnish plates of choux buns with sprigs of parsley before serving. *Makes 40*

Seafood Gougère

2 quantities Choux pastry (see page 108)
grated rind of 2 lemons
450 g/1 lb cod fillets, skinned
1 (250-g/9-oz) can mussels in brine, drained
225 g/8 oz peeled prawns
50 g/2 oz butter
1 small onion, sliced
2 cloves garlic, crushed
1 tablespoon plain flour
250 ml/8 fl oz dry white wine
2 tablespoons chopped parsley
salt and freshly ground black pepper

Make the pastry according to the recipe instructions and beat in the lemon rind. Place the pastry in a piping bag fitted with a large star nozzle and pipe swirls round the edge of a 1.4-litre/2½-pint oven-proof dish.

Remove any bones from the fish and cut it into bite-sized chunks. Mix with the mussels and prawns. Melt the butter in a small saucepan, add the onion and garlic and cook until soft but not browned. Stir in the flour and gradually add the wine. Sprinkle half of the parsley into the sauce and season generously.

Place half of the fish mixture in the middle of the dish and pour over half of the sauce. Place in a hot oven (220°C, 425°F, Gas Mark 7) for 20 minutes. Add the remaining fish mixture and sauce and return to a moderately hot oven (190°C, 375°F, Gas Mark 5) and bake for a further 30 minutes. Sprinkle the reserved parsley over the dish before serving. *Serves 6*

Variation
Savoury Mince Gougère: (*Illustrated on page 35*) The choux ring may be filled with a savoury mince mixture made by cooking 450 g/1 lb minced beef with 1 onion, finely chopped. When lightly browned, season to taste and add 300 ml/½ pint beef stock. Thicken with 1 tablespoon cornflour mixed with 1 tablespoon cold water. Place in the choux ring and cook as above.

Cheesy Cauliflower Puffs with Curried Egg Dip

2 quantities Choux pastry (see page 108)
100 g/4 oz Cheddar cheese, finely grated
salt and freshly ground black pepper
225 g/8 oz cauliflower florets
oil for deep frying
Sauce
50 g/2 oz butter
1 large onion, finely chopped
2 cloves garlic, crushed
3 tablespoons grated root ginger
2 teaspoons concentrated curry paste
300 ml/$\frac{1}{2}$ pint mayonnaise
4 hard-boiled eggs, finely chopped
1 tablespoon chopped parsley or chives

Make the pastry according to the recipe instructions, adding the cheese and seasoning to taste after beating in the eggs. Coat the cauliflower florets in the pastry, using two teaspoons. Deep fry in the oil until crisp and golden brown. Drain on absorbent kitchen paper and keep hot.

To prepare the sauce, melt the butter in a frying pan. Add the onion, garlic and ginger and sauté until the onion is soft but not browned. Remove from the heat, cool slightly and mix in the curry paste, mayonnaise, eggs and chopped parsley or chives. Serve the hot cauliflower puffs with the chilled sauce. *Serves 4*

Chicken and Asparagus Ring

1 quantity Choux pastry (see page 108)
50 g/2 oz mature Cheddar cheese, finely grated
350 g/12 oz cooked chicken, diced
225 g/8 oz cooked asparagus, coarsely chopped
salt and freshly ground black pepper
1 teaspoon lemon juice
150 ml/$\frac{1}{4}$ pint double cream
150 ml/$\frac{1}{4}$ pint mayonnaise
1 tablespoon chopped lemon balm or parsley
450 g/1 lb tomatoes, peeled and quartered
2 tablespoons olive oil
1 clove garlic, crushed
2 spring onions, finely chopped

Grease a baking tray. Make the pastry according to the recipe instructions and beat in the grated cheese. Place the pastry in a piping bag fitted with a 2.5-cm/1-inch plain or star nozzle. Pipe a 20-cm/8-inch double ring of pastry on to the baking tray. Bake in a hot oven (220°C, 425°F, Gas Mark 7) for 15 minutes then reduce the temperature to moderately hot (190°C, 375°F, Gas Mark 5) and cook for a further 30 minutes. Split the ring immediately it is taken from the oven to allow any steam to escape and cool on a wire rack.

Mix the chicken and asparagus together and season generously. Mix the lemon juice with the lightly-whipped cream and mayonnaise. Add the lemon balm or parsley and add to the chicken mixture. Fill the cooled choux ring with this mixture and place on a serving dish.

Mix the tomatoes with the olive oil, garlic and spring onions and pile in the centre of the ring. *Serves 6–8*

Variation
Use 350 g/12 oz cooked smoked ham, finely chopped instead of the chicken.

Lamb Curry with Banana Puffs

(Illustrated on page 91)
100 g/4 oz butter
3 onions, finely chopped
5 tablespoons grated root ginger
450 g/1 lb minced lamb
1 small egg, lightly beaten
salt and freshly ground black pepper
3 cloves garlic, crushed
1 teaspoon ground coriander
1 teaspoon ground cumin
2 teaspoons turmeric
2 cardamoms
1 teaspoon chilli powder
150 ml/$\frac{1}{4}$ pint chicken stock
300 ml/$\frac{1}{2}$ pint natural yogurt
$\frac{1}{2}$ quantity Choux pastry (see page 108)
grated rind and juice of 1 lemon
5 bananas
chopped parsley to garnish

Grease a baking tray. Melt half the butter in a frying pan and gently
sauté one of the onions and 2 tablespoons of the grated root ginger
until soft but not browned. Add to the minced lamb with the egg
and mix well. Season and shape into meatballs using wet hands.
Melt the remaining butter in the frying pan, add the meatballs and
sauté until just brown. Remove and sauté the remaining onion,
garlic and the ginger in the remaining butter until soft. Add the
coriander, cumin, turmeric, cardamoms and chilli powder and cook
for a few minutes. Stir in the stock and yogurt and season to taste.
Add the meatballs and bring the curry to the boil. Simmer gently,
covered, for 30–40 minutes.

Meanwhile prepare the choux buns. Make the pastry according to
the recipe instructions, adding the lemon rind after beating in the
egg. Place the pastry in a piping bag fitted with a 1-cm/$\frac{1}{2}$-inch plain

nozzle and pipe small choux buns on to the baking tray. Bake in a hot oven (220°C, 425°F, Gas Mark 7) for 15–20 minutes. Make a slit in the side of each bun immediately they are taken from the oven to allow any steam to escape.

Peel the bananas, cut into bite-sized pieces and sprinkle with lemon juice. Place a piece of banana in each bun. Transfer the curry to a serving dish and arrange the buns on top. Reheat in the oven for 3–5 minutes and serve sprinkled with chopped parsley. *Serves 6*

Bacon and Sweetcorn Aigrettes

I quantity Choux pastry (see page 108)
1 (198-g/7-oz) can sweetcorn, drained
175 g/6 oz lean bacon, rind removed and finely chopped
oil for deep frying

Make the pastry according to the recipe instructions. Beat in the sweetcorn and bacon. Deep fry small spoonfuls of the mixture in the oil, a few at a time, until well puffed and golden brown. Drain on absorbent kitchen paper and serve hot or cold. *Makes 20–30*

Variations

Chicken Aigrettes: Add 350 g/12 oz finely-chopped cooked chicken instead of the sweetcorn and bacon. Cook as above.

Cheese and Onion Aigrettes: Add 1 small, finely-chopped onion and 50 g/2 oz finely-grated mature Cheddar cheese to the pastry instead of the bacon and sweetcorn. Cook as above. These are best served hot or warm as they toughen and become slightly greasy on cooling (due to the extra fat content included in the cheese).

Lattice-topped Pork

(Illustrated on page 74)
1 large aubergine
2 teaspoons salt
50 g/2 oz butter
2 cloves garlic, crushed
1 large onion, sliced
2 large courgettes, sliced
450 g/1 lb tomatoes, peeled
450 g/1 lb minced pork
1 small onion, chopped
1 teaspoon powdered sage
grated rind of 1 orange
salt and freshly ground black pepper
1 tablespoon plain flour
300 ml/$\frac{1}{2}$ pint dry cider
1 quantity Choux pastry (see page 108)
50 g/2 oz Cheddar cheese, grated

Cut the aubergine into chunks and sprinkle with the salt. Leave to stand for 20–30 minutes in a colander then rinse and drain well. Melt the butter in a pan, add the garlic, sliced onion and courgettes. Cook, stirring continuously, for a few minutes. Transfer to a 1.75-litre/3-pint ovenproof dish. Slice the tomatoes and arrange over the vegetables.

Place the pork and chopped onion in a pan, cook slowly until well browned. Add the sage and orange rind and season generously. Gradually stir in the flour and add the cider. Bring to the boil then pour over the tomatoes.

Make the pastry according to the recipe instructions and beat in the grated cheese. Place the pastry in a piping bag fitted with a small star nozzle and pipe a lattice over the pork. Use any remaining pastry to pipe tiny buns round the edge of the dish. Bake in a moderately hot oven (200°C, 400°F, Gas Mark 6) for 40 minutes or until the pastry is well puffed and golden. Serve immediately. *Serves 6*

Potato Puffs

(Illustrated on page 92)
An interesting way to serve potatoes.

I quantity Choux pastry (see page 108)
350 g/12 oz potatoes, boiled and mashed
I teaspoon grated nutmeg
100 g/4 oz black olives, stoned and finely chopped
2 tablespoons chopped parsley
salt and freshly ground black pepper
oil for deep frying

Make the pastry according to the recipe instructions. Add the potatoes, nutmeg, olives and parsley to the pastry, beating well. Season to taste. Heat the oil in a deep frying pan and drop spoonfuls of the mixture into the hot oil. Deep fry until crisp and golden brown, about 3–5 minutes. *Makes 25*

Variation
Replace the olives and parsley with 75 g/3 oz finely-grated Cheddar cheese.

Melba Puffs

1 quantity Choux pastry (see page 108)
4 peaches or 1 (411-g/14½-oz) can peach halves
1 (625-ml/22-fl oz) tub vanilla ice cream
Melba sauce
350 g/12 oz fresh or frozen raspberries
100 g/4 oz castor sugar

Grease a baking tray. Make the pastry according to the recipe instructions. Place the pastry in a piping bag fitted with a 1.5-cm/¾-inch plain nozzle and pipe eight large choux buns on to the baking tray. Bake in a hot oven (220°C, 425°F, Gas Mark 7) for 15 minutes, then reduce the heat to moderate (180°C, 350°F, Gas Mark 4) and cook for a further 15–20 minutes.

Meanwhile prepare the Melba sauce. Cook the raspberries with the sugar for a few minutes then reduce to a purée in a liquidiser. Press through a sieve to remove any seeds. Peel the peaches, cut in half and remove the stones. Alternatively, drain the canned peaches. Cut the choux buns in half, place 2–3 tablespoons of ice cream in the bottom of each bun. Cover with half a peach and place the tops of the buns in place. Serve with the Melba sauce. *Makes 8*

Raspberry Buns

1 quantity Choux pastry (see page 108)
225 g/8 oz fresh or frozen raspberries
100 g/4 oz curd or cream cheese
20 g/¾ oz castor sugar
150 ml/¼ pint double cream
icing sugar to decorate

Grease a baking tray. Make the pastry according to the recipe instructions and place in a piping bag fitted with a 1.5-cm/¾-inch plain nozzle. Pipe eight large choux buns on to the baking tray and bake in a hot oven (220°C, 425°F, Gas Mark 7) for 15 minutes, then reduce the heat to moderate (180°C, 350°F, Gas Mark 4) and cook for a further 15–20 minutes. Split the buns immediately they come out of the oven to allow any steam to escape.

Meanwhile prepare the filling. Add the raspberries to the curd or cream cheese with the castor sugar and 2 tablespoons of the cream. Stir well. Whip the remainder of the cream and fold into the cheese and raspberry mixture. Use this mixture to fill the choux buns. Dust with icing sugar and serve. *Makes 8*

Variation

Coffee and Walnut Buns: (*Illustrated on page 101*) The buns may be filled with a coffee and walnut cream instead of the raspberry mixture. Fold 50 g/2 oz chopped walnuts and 4 teaspoons sweetened coffee essence into 300 ml/½ pint whipped double cream and fill as above.

Orange Choux Ring

1 quantity Choux pastry (see page 108)
300 ml/½ pint double cream
grated rind of 1 orange
25 g/1 oz icing sugar
4 oranges, peeled and sliced
175 g/6 oz castor sugar
100 ml/4 fl oz cold water

Grease a baking tray. Make the pastry according to the recipe instructions, place in a piping bag fitted with a 1.5-cm/¾-inch plain nozzle and pipe an 18-cm/7-inch ring on to the baking tray. Alternatively, neatly arrange the paste using two spoons. Use any remaining pastry to pipe six small choux buns. Bake in a hot oven (220°C, 425°F, Gas Mark 7) for 15 minutes, then reduce the temperature to moderate (180°C, 350°F, Gas Mark 4) and continue to cook for a further 15–20 minutes. Split the ring to allow any steam to escape and cool on a wire rack.

Meanwhile prepare the filling. Whip the cream, orange rind and icing sugar together. Remove any pips and excess pith from the oranges and arrange half of them on the base of the ring. Place a little cream in each of the buns and place the remainder on top of the oranges. Arrange the remaining oranges over it. Place the second piece of pastry on top and carefully arrange the buns around the ring.

Make a caramel by mixing the sugar and water together in a saucepan. Heat until the sugar dissolves then bring to the boil and cook rapidly until a light caramel is reached. Gently pour a thin stream of caramel over the choux ring. Serve within 2 hours of filling. *Serves 6–8*

Variation
Cherry Choux Ring: (*Illustrated on page 101*) Alternatively, the ring may be filled with whipped cream, flavoured with a little canned cherry juice and topped with canned cherries. Coat with caramel as above and sprinkle the buns with chopped nuts.

Black Cherry Choux Gâteau

450 g/1 lb pitted black cherries
6 tablespoons brandy
50 g/2 oz castor sugar
1 quantity Choux pastry (see page 108)
300 ml/½ pint double cream
icing sugar to decorate

Grease a baking tray. Soak the cherries in the brandy and sugar for 3 hours.

Make the pastry according to the recipe instructions, place in a piping bag fitted with a 1.5-cm/¾-inch plain nozzle and pipe an 18-cm/7-inch round on to the baking tray. Bake in a hot oven (220°C, 425°F, Gas Mark 7) for 15 minutes, then reduce the oven temperature to moderate (180°C, 350°F, Gas Mark 4) and continue cooking for a further 15–20 minutes. Split the choux round in half immediately it is removed from the oven, to allow any steam to escape. Cool on a wire rack.

Meanwhile prepare the filling. Whip the cream together with the juice from the cherries. Stir in the cherries and use to fill the choux gâteau. Decorate with a little sifted icing sugar. *Serves 6–8*

Variation
Strawberry Choux Gâteau: *(Illustrated on page 101)* Alternatively, the gâteau may be filled and topped with a strawberry and cream mixture. Fold 225 g/8 oz sliced strawberries into 300 ml/½ pint whipped cream and use to fill and top the choux gâteau. Decorate with halved strawberries and flaked toasted almonds.

Banana Buns

1 quantity Choux pastry (see page 108)
150 ml/$\frac{1}{4}$ pint double cream
2 tablespoons rum
2 tablespoons castor sugar
2 bananas, chopped
225 g/8 oz plain chocolate, melted

Grease a baking tray. Make the pastry according to the recipe instructions and place in a piping bag fitted with a 1.5-cm/$\frac{3}{4}$-inch plain nozzle. Pipe eight buns on to the baking tray and bake in a hot oven (220°C, 425°F, Gas Mark 7) for 15–20 minutes. Split the buns immediately they are removed from the oven to allow any steam to escape. Cool on a wire rack.

Meanwhile prepare the filling. Whip the cream with the rum and sugar then add the bananas. Fill each bun with the filling and top with a little melted chocolate. Serve within 2 hours of filling. *Makes 14*

Fruit Aigrettes

These aigrettes are the ideal teatime treat. Other canned or fresh fruit can be substituted for the pineapple, for example, try coarsely-chopped canned apricot, apple or banana.

I quantity Choux pastry (see page 108)
50 g/2 oz castor sugar
grated rind of I orange
I (439-g/15½-oz) can pineapple rings
oil for deep frying
icing sugar to decorate

Make the pastry according to the recipe instructions. Add the sugar and orange rind. Drain the pineapple and dry on absorbent kitchen paper then chop finely. Add to the pastry.

Heat the oil to 185°C/360°F and fry spoonfuls of the choux pastry mixture until well puffed and golden brown, about 3–5 minutes. Drain on absorbent kitchen paper. Sift a little icing sugar over the aigrettes before serving while they are still very warm. *Makes 20*

Gingered Profiteroles

(Illustrated on pages 102–3)
1 quantity Choux pastry (see page 108)
300 ml/½ pint double cream
50 g/2 oz sugar
150 ml/¼ pint water
pared rind of 1 orange
150 ml/¼ pint ginger wine
2 pieces preserved ginger, chopped

Grease two baking trays. Make the pastry according to the recipe instructions and pipe or spoon 20 small buns well apart on to the baking trays. Bake in a hot oven (220°C, 425°F, Gas Mark 7) for 15–20 minutes. Make a slit in each bun immediately they are removed from the oven to allow any steam to escape. Cool on a wire rack.

Whip the cream until stiff and use to fill the buns. Place the sugar, water and orange rind in a saucepan, bring to the boil and cook for 10–15 minutes until a thick syrup is formed but the mixture has not caramelised. Remove from the heat and carefully stir in the ginger wine and chopped ginger. Pour the sauce over the profiteroles to serve. *Makes 20*

Variation
Chocolate Profiteroles: *(Illustrated on page 104)* The profiteroles may be served with a traditional chocolate sauce. Make the sauce by melting 225 g/8 oz plain chocolate with 3 tablespoons golden syrup in a basin over boiling water.

Lemon Éclairs

I quantity Choux pastry (see page 108)
150 ml/$\frac{1}{4}$ pint double cream
225 g/8 oz lemon curd
50 g/2 oz butter
100 g/4 oz plain chocolate
juice of $\frac{1}{2}$ lemon

Grease two baking trays. Make the pastry according to the recipe instructions and place in a piping bag fitted with a 1.5-cm/$\frac{3}{4}$-inch plain nozzle. Pipe 12 éclairs on to the baking trays and bake in a hot oven (220°C, 425°F, Gas Mark 7) for 15 minutes then reduce the temperature to moderately hot (190°C, 375°F, Gas Mark 5) and cook for a further 25–30 minutes. Remove from the baking trays and make a slit into each éclair immediately they are removed from the oven to allow any steam to escape. Cool on a wire rack.

Whip the cream until stiff and gently stir in the lemon curd. Use to fill the cooled éclairs. Melt the butter, chocolate and lemon juice in a basin over a saucepan of very hot water and use to coat the tops of the éclairs. *Makes 12*

Index